A Birder's Guide to Montgomery County, Maryland

**The Montgomery
County Chapter
of the Maryland
Ornithological Society**

Illustrations by Michael O'Brien.
Graphic design by Gemma Radko.

Second printing 2002.

ISBN 1–930867–00–X

This guide is dedicated
to the memory of

CLAUDIA WILDS

who, with her passion for accuracy,
her high standards of birding ethics, and
her admirable guide to bird-finding,
gave us a model to follow.

Table of Contents

A Birder's Guide to Montgomery County, MD

Foreword

As someone who owns and makes enthusiastic use of more than 100 "bird-finding" guides to all parts of the U.S. and lands beyond, I find it especially thrilling to pen a foreword to my own county's new guide. Despite explosive suburban growth since World War II, Montgomery County—just north of our nation's capital—still possesses much to attract and hold the interest of the birder. Thanks to the work of committed conservationists, ordinary citizens, and responsible public officials, a patchwork of local, regional, state, and federal lands offers birds and birders refuge amid the suburban sprawl. We hope users of this guide—county residents and visitors alike—will get to know them and learn of the delightful richness of bird life that they shelter.

Our chapter's effort was spurred partly by the publication in the 1990s of useful and attractive guides by our neighbors to the north: Frederick, Howard, and Baltimore Counties. We have emulated some of their excellent ideas and offer them our thanks for being pioneers. In mid-1999, Linda Friedland, then the Montgomery Chapter president, appointed a steering committee to plan and drive the project, under the leadership of Coordinator Rick Sussman. The full committee consisted of Rick, Linda (editor-in-chief), John Bjerke (checklist revision), Rob Gibbs (maps), Paul O'Brien (species accounts), Gemma Radko (graphic design and layout), Janet Millenson, Cyndie Loeper, Frank Witebsky, and myself. We are particularly pleased to be able to feature the striking art of former Montgomery County resident Michael O'Brien. Many of the site descriptions first appeared in *The Chat*, the chapter's newsletter, where they benefited from skilled editing by Lydia Schindler and others.

This all-volunteer project relied on members and others who contributed in small but important ways. Thanks go to those who spent time visiting the sites, checking mileage, providing data, and helping with the initial proofreading: Suzanne Dater, Lou DeMouy, Dan Eberly, Sid Friedland, David and Helen Gray, Jim Green, Jane Hill, Ann Lucy, H. Michael Mogil, Kathy Neugebauer, Lola Oberman, Dillon Rankin, Grace-Louise and George Rickard, Paul Schindler,

Karen Stewart, Johanna Thompson, David Winer, and Sandy Zimmerman. Thanks also to Chapter Treasurer Howard Lefkowitz for serving as a dynamic business manager. Special thanks to Janet Millenson, Lydia Schindler, and Ann Weeks for the countless hours spent in the laborious task of final proofreading.

We are also grateful to chapter members who contributed to the Claudia Wilds Fund; to the late Ann Kennedy for her bequest to the chapter; and to those who made an additional contribution in Ann's memory—all of whom helped finance this endeavor.

Good birding!

— Michael Bowen
President, 2000-01

Using the Guide

When the Site Guide Steering Committee began work on this book over two years ago, our aim was to provide clear and accurate descriptions of Montgomery County's best birding sites for residents and visitors alike. At the same time, we decided to make the book as user-friendly as possible by including several cross-referencing systems that take the place of an index.

The core of the book focuses on "where to go"—sites throughout the county that have proven productive over the years. Within this section are two sub-sections: **Major Sites** and **Little Treasures**. Most of the Major Sites are large, publicly owned parks that require at least a half day for full exploration; Little Treasures are smaller, easily accessible spots where a birder can spend a profitable hour or two. All major sites feature the Site-at-a-Glance box: a capsule of information about terrain, amenities, and so forth.

In addition to where to go, the birder needs to know "when to go"—the best times to look for common (and uncommon) birds. **The Birding Year in Montgomery County** is a month-by-month account highlighting many species' first appearance, likely habitat, and period of greatest abundance. A useful companion to the Birding Year is the **Quick Locator**, in which families of birds—waterfowl, warblers, or sparrows—are keyed to specific sites. The **Species Accounts** provide further details about all species recorded in the county and the latest **Montgomery County Checklist of Birds** itemizes abundance and breeding data.

We hope that all aspects of this book will augment your birding experiences and that, in the process, you will make discoveries of your own. But before you venture forth into the field, guide in hand, a few cautionary notes:

- Y Remember that odometer readings may vary as much as 0.1 mile.

- Y Use caution when driving on narrow back roads that are heavily trafficked.

Y Many sites—in particular the C&O Canal—have some isolated stretches. Common sense dictates that it is always best to bird with a friend or in a small group. You may want to carry a cell phone.

Y Avoid leaving personal property visible in parked cars, especially in C&O lots.

Y Do not trespass on private land.

Y Be aware that grassy fields (even in winter months) can harbor ticks bearing Lyme and other diseases, and take appropriate precautions.

At the time of publication we had checked (and re-checked) driving directions and trail descriptions. Still, one should keep in mind that continuing "progress" may affect access to—or the very existence of—some sites, particularly the Little Treasures. As we hope to revise this book in the future, please send feedback to Site Guide, Montgomery County Chapter, Maryland Ornithological Society, P.O. Box 59639, Potomac, MD 20859-9639.

— Linda Friedland
Editor-in-Chief

Terms and Abbreviations

Black Hill: Birders' term for Black Hill Regional Park's Little Seneca Lake.

The canal: Chesapeake and Ohio (C&O) Canal.

Hughes Hollow: Birders' term for McKee-Beshers WMA.

M-NCPPC: Maryland–National Capital Park and Planning Commission.

MP: Milepost; mileage measurements along the canal towpath.

PEPCO: Potomac Electric Power Company.

WMA: Wildlife Management Area.

WSSC: Washington Suburban Sanitary Commission.

Montgomery County, Maryland, sited in the Mid-Atlantic states and immediately adjacent to the nation's capital, lies almost entirely on the Piedmont Plateau. Its low, rolling hills are bounded on the south and west by the Potomac River and on the north and east by the Patuxent River.

The county's 497 square miles encompass a wide variety of natural habitats. The area contains several manmade lakes, many ponds, and a few vital wetlands. More than 1,500 miles of streams run through the county, feeding into the Northwest Branch of the Anacostia River, upper Rock Creek, Paint Branch Creek, and Seneca Creek, as well as the Potomac and Patuxent Rivers. The Potomac River in Montgomery County is studded with some 136 islands, a fourth of them larger than five acres. The waters of the Potomac, up to the high tide line on the Virginia shore, officially belong to Maryland.

For the most part, stream banks are protected with rich riparian forest. Deciduous hardwood forests are typical—sycamore, maple, willow, elm, cottonwood, white ash, green ash, hickory, walnut, paw paw, and pin oak. Virtually all forested areas are second-growth, though some are quite old.

With a population in excess of 870,000, once-rural Montgomery County necessarily includes highly developed city/suburban areas. By virtue of nationally recognized programs in agricultural preservation and park planning and development, it also boasts large swaths of farmland (more than 90,000 acres) and parkland (more than 45,000 acres).

Thirty-five miles of the Chesapeake and Ohio Canal National Historical Park run along the county's western edge. State lands falling within county boundaries include sections of Patuxent River State Park, Seneca Creek State Park, and McKee-Beshers Wildlife Management Area. The county is home to five regional parks plus scores of smaller ones, including six nondeveloped conservation parks and more than two dozen nondeveloped stream valley parks.

With its varied habitats, the county regularly attracts some 251 species of birds—either year-round residents, winter visitors, migratory pass-throughs, or summer breeders: 121 species are known to breed in the county. In addition, county lists identify 68 accidentals that have been seen only a few times in the past two decades. The area is particularly rich in woodpeckers: the local Christmas Count holds the national all-time highs for Downy Woodpecker, for Yellow-shafted Northern Flicker, and for our "Chapter Bird," the Pileated Woodpecker.

—*Lydia Schindler*

A Word about Weather

Montgomery County enjoys the generally moderate temperatures typical of a middle-latitude climate. However, summer's characteristically high relative humidity can make hot days feel even hotter. Spring and fall, with lower humidity and less precipitation, offer the most pleasant birding.

The county's annual rainfall of 40 inches is distributed fairly uniformly year-round. In late spring and throughout the summer, widely scattered afternoon thunderstorms can bring torrential downpours and dangerous lightning.

Total snowfall averages about 18 inches, but is heavier the farther north and west one goes in the county. It is not unusual for areas near Washington, DC, to be awash in rain, while the more northern and western parts of the county can be buried under a foot of snow. In between, a "winter mix" of sleet, freezing rain and/or snow can create hazardous driving conditions.

A History of Birding in Montgomery County

It is appropriate that this history of birding in Montgomery County be written by Dr. Donald Messersmith, who has himself contributed substantially to that story. Don is a retired professor of entomology at the University of Maryland, where he taught entomology, ornithology, and environmental education. His "Field Study" courses in ornithology, taught for 36 years at the Audubon Naturalist Society and in conjunction with the Graduate School, USDA, have created a cadre of knowledgeable bird enthusiasts who have greatly enriched the ranks of local birders.

The earliest records of Montgomery County birds are difficult to determine, because they are mingled with reports from the adjacent District of Columbia and from other parts of Maryland. A rather vague reference to a quote by the Rev. Andrew White in 1677 stating that parrots abound in winter in Baltimore County might suggest Carolina Parakeets in what is now Montgomery County.

Probably the earliest serious birding was done by Dr. Elliott Coues and Dr. D. Webster Prentiss between 1858 and 1862 when they were medical students at Columbian University. They wrote that "the country all about was as primitive as the most enthusiastic naturalist could desire." An article based on their extensive notes and titled "List of the Birds of the District of Columbia, etc." in the 16th Annual Report of the Smithsonian Institution for 1861 [399-421, 1862] enumerated 226 species.

In 1879, Coues prepared a "List of Birds ascertained to occur within a radius of fifty miles around Fort McHenry Md.," in "Zoology of Vicinity of Post," *Ornithology*, 1879. This list contains 233 species. In 1883, Coues and Prentiss published a second edition of their "List," completely revised and rewritten, which appeared in the *Bulletin of the United States National Museum* [No. 26]. The list, entitled "Avifauna Columbiana: Being a List of Birds Ascertained to Inhabit the District of Columbia, with the Times of Arrival and Departure of such as Are Non-Residents, and Brief Notes of Habits, etc." It includes some references to birds collected in Montgomery County, and the attached map stretches as far as Rockville in the northwest and the Patuxent River to the northeast.

In 1895, Frank C. Kirkwood published "A List of the Birds of Maryland" in the *Transactions of the Maryland Academy of Sciences* [2: 241-382]. Although most of the records are from the Baltimore area, there are a few references to birds collected elsewhere, including some from a colleague in Kinsington [*sic*]. Kirkwood lists several sightings of Passenger Pigeons as late as 1893. He also has a reference from *Audubon* [IV, 124] that the Ivory-billed Woodpecker is seen occasionally in Maryland (Montgomery County?).

Lucy Warner Maynard's 1898 book *Birds of Washington and Vicinity* mentions several Montgomery County localities, including Chevy Chase, Takoma Park, Forest Glen, Kensington, and Rockville. She states, "Passenger Pigeons are now very irregular in September and October."

Several organizations played a role in the evolution of birding in Montgomery County. The Biological Society, formed in 1880, published lists that included Montgomery County birds. One of these, published by May Thacher Cooke in 1929 in the *Proceedings of the Biological Society of Washington* [42: 1-80], contains 287 species. The Natural History Society of Maryland, formed in 1929, had an active ornithological program and published bird records. Other records of Montgomery County birds are scattered in the literature. However, it was not until 1958 that we find rather complete coverage of the subject with frequent mention of Montgomery County. This came with the publication of "Birds of Maryland and the District of Columbia," by Robert E. Stewart and Chandler S. Robbins, in *North American Fauna* [No. 62, 1958]. Stewart and Robbins also list many people who carried out field studies in the early part of the 20th century.

The Audubon Naturalist Society of the District of Columbia (now of the Central Atlantic States) was formed in 1897. An 1898 list identifies 290 species for Washington, D.C., and vicinity. The society's first official birding trip to Montgomery County occurred on May 13, 1901, when a "Field Meeting" was held at Forest Glen Seminary. As reported in the *Washington Star*, the meeting was led by Henry Olds and Arthur H. Howell, and the participants were 13 women (probably students in their bird class). The paper reported that 50-60 specimens were "inspected." In 1908, Dr. C. W. Richmond prepared a list called "Birds of Chevy Chase" that included 42 permanent resident species, 46 summer residents, 40 spring and fall migrants, and 10 winter residents.

A mimeographed, four-page leaflet called *Audubon Bird Bulletin* No. 2, May 1945, by Richard Tousey, is entitled "Where to See Birds in the District of Columbia Region" and includes the C&O Canal in Montgomery County. The April 1946 issue of the *Wood Thrush*, the first journal of the Audubon Naturalist Society (ANS), reports that the first Breeding Bird Census was conducted on April 14, 1946. Led by Robert E. Stewart, Chandler S. Robbins, and B.M. McHenry, the participants covered the area from Sycamore Island to Minnehaha Creek. In May of 1946, there were trips to Langley Park and a "Big Day Trip" to Seneca. That year's Christmas Count, on December 21, extended into part of Montgomery County.

In 1947, the Audubon Naturalist Society published the first edition of *A Field List of Birds of the District of Columbia Region*, compiled by John W. Aldrich, Irston R. Barnes, Roger Tory Peterson, Chandler S. Robbins, Robert E. Stewart, and Richard Tousey. Two Montgomery County sites—the C&O Canal and Seneca—are listed. The Second Edition (1961) added the Buckeystown-Dickerson area, and the Revised Edition (1968) included Hughes Hollow and Great Falls Park.

Two other ANS publications were *Montgomery County Localities: Where Birds Live. Habitats in the Middle Atlantic States*, edited by Shirley A. Briggs and Chandler S. Robbins, 1951; and *Washington—City in the Woods*, edited by Shirley A. Briggs, 1954. The latter contains short articles by several birders who tell of their favorite birding spots, including the Potomac River and the C&O Canal.

When the Maryland Ornithological Society (MOS) was organized on April 9, 1945, as an offshoot of the Natural History Society of Maryland, record-keeping became more organized. In the May–June 1947 issue of *Maryland Birdlife*, W. Bryant Terrell reports on bird activity at his feeding shelf in Takoma Park, the first reference to Montgomery County birds to appear in that publication. The first recorded county Christmas Count was the Seneca Count of 1955-56 when, in ten party-hours, the participants saw 32 species. This count has since been joined by the Triadelphia, Sugarloaf, and DC Counts.

In March 1968, the Maryland Ornithological Society published *Field List of the Birds of Maryland*, by Chandler S. Robbins and Willet T. Van Velzen. Known as the "Yellow Book," it listed 329 species and included five specific Montgomery County birding spots. The second edition by Chandler S. Robbins and Danny Bystrak, published in April 1977, listed 374 species. By the time the third edition appeared in May 1996, the number of species had risen to 399. The *Field List* also lists each bird by county, and of the 399 Maryland species, 319 have been reported in Montgomery County in recent years.

Under the leadership of W. Bryant Terrell, a chapter of MOS called the Takoma Park Nature Club was formed in 1951 and remained active until 1962. Another chapter, the Rossmoor Bird Club, existed from December 1968 until 1972. These groups organized field trips and kept some records of Montgomery County birds.

From 1964 to 1969 Carl W. Carlson, a resident of Bethesda, wrote a series of 19 bird-finding articles in the ANS publication *The Atlantic Naturalist*. An article on Montgomery County, published in January 1965, described "Travilah, Seneca, and Sycamore Landing, Maryland." It was about this time that a group of active birders who were members of MOS and ANS came together to form the Montgomery County Chapter (MCC) of MOS. Founded and organized by Carl W. Carlson and Sarah Baker, the new chapter first met in October 1964. In March 1965, its first annual meeting drew 63 charter members. On March 21, 1965, Carl Carlson led the new chapter's first field trip, along the C&O Canal from Potomac to Sycamore Landing. Its newsletter (now called *The Chat*) first appeared in 1967. Today, membership stands at 300.

Around 1968, someone (possibly Carl Carlson) prepared a hand-printed and -colored "Bird Checklist for Montgomery Co. MD." It lists most of the common birds (147 species) reported for the county up to that time and shows their occurrence by quarters with simple bar graphs. The 1995 *Montgomery County Checklist*, prepared by a committee headed by Norm Saunders, with John Bjerke and Julie Kelly, and with assistance from 21 members, contains 317 species, including 65 accidentals. In 2001, John Bjerke, once more with the assistance of local birders, updated the checklist.

The sole MOS Sanctuary in Montgomery County, called "Adventure," is located on Glen Road in Potomac. From fall 1972 through spring 1995, MCC charter members Margaret and Morrill (Don) Donnald managed an ambitious bird-banding program on the 16-acre property. With the help of some 180 volunteers, they amassed a wealth of information on patterns of bird migration. A new banding program—this time targeting nesting birds—began in May 2000. Chapter member Gemma Radko heads the summer operation.

Montgomery County, with its large cadre of competent birders, has twice served as a testing ground for new bird-censusing projects. In January and February 1970, Montgomery County and portions of five other counties tested a new winter bird survey technique developed by Chandler S. Robbins and reported by him in *Maryland Birdlife* [26:11-20, 1970]. A much more ambitious project was the Maryland breeding bird atlas; here, too, the techniques were initially tried out in Montgomery County, as reported by M. Kathleen Klimkiewicz in *Maryland Birdlife* [28:130-41, 1972]. A second article, by M. Kathleen Klimkiewicz and Joanne K. Solem, "The Breeding Bird Atlas of Montgomery and Howard Counties, Maryland," appeared in *Maryland Birdlife* in 1978 [34:3-39, 1978].

Building on these studies, the statewide atlas project got under way in 1983. For five years, under the guidance of county coordinators, some 797 volunteers recorded breeding species in their "blocks" (the state was divided into 239 blocks, each 2.83 by 3.37 miles). By the end of three years, under the direction of County Coordinator Keith D. Van Ness, Jr., Montgomery County's effort was judged the best in the state, with almost all areas covered and an average of 60 to 70 species per block. The census results were published in 1996 in the *Atlas of the Breeding Birds of Maryland and the District of Columbia*, by Chandler S. Robbins, senior editor, and Eirik A. T. Blom, project coordinator [University of Pittsburgh Press]. The resulting distribution maps show 120 species as confirmed breeders in Montgomery County, with an additional seven as probable breeders.

During the 1980s, the late Claudia Wilds, an internationally recognized authority on birds and a former president of the Montgomery County chapter, developed a book that would become an invaluable

guide to local birding: *Finding Birds in the National Capital Area*. This
meticulously researched and comprehensive guide set the standard
for all guidebooks to follow, including this one. Published in 1989
and revised in 1992, the book describes good birding sites in
Maryland, Virginia, Delaware, and North Carolina and includes a
number of areas in Montgomery County.

—*Don Messersmith*

	Location	Waterfowl	Shorebirds & waders	Woodpeckers &	Thrushes & forest species	Vireos & warblers	Sparrows
Major Sites	Black Hill	X			X		
	C&O Canal	X			X	X	
	Lake Needwood/Rock Creek				X	X	X
	Layhill Park			X	X	X	X
	Little Bennett			X	X	X	X
	McKee-Beshers	X		X	X	X	X
	Meadowside	X			X	X	
	Rachel Carson					X	X
	Seneca Creek	X			X	X	
	Triadelphia Lake Road	X	X		X	X	X
Little Treasures	Ag. History Farm Park					X	X
	Back Roads		X				X
	Blockhouse Point				X		X
	Brookside Nature Center				X	X	X
	Croydon Creek				X	X	X
	Duck Ponds	X					X
	Four Gems along Patuxent	X	X		X	X	
	Gunners Lake	X					
	Little Falls Branch				X	X	X
	Locust Grove				X	X	X
	Maydale Park		X		X	X	
	Meditation Park				X	X	X
	Sligo Creek				X	X	
	Upper Watts Branch				X	X	
	Woottons Mill				X		X

MAJOR SITES

American Redstart

MOB
'95

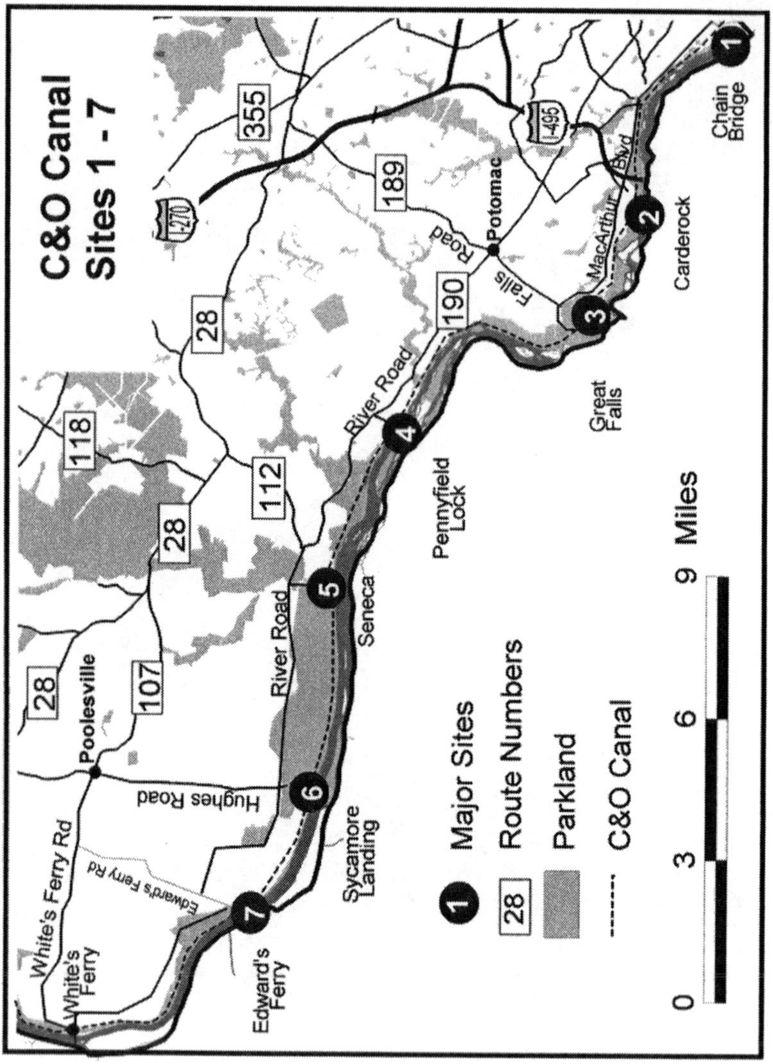
C&O Canal
Sites 1 - 7
Major Sites
Route Numbers
Parkland
C&O Canal
0
3
6
9 Miles
White's Ferry Rd
White's Ferry
Edward's Ferry Rd
Edward's Ferry
Poolesville
Hughes Road
Sycamore Landing
River Road
Seneca
Pennyfield Lock
River Road
Great Falls
Falls Road
Potomac
MacArthur Blvd
Carderock
Chain Bridge
28
107
28
112
118
28
190
189
270
355
495

C&O Canal National Historical Park

R unning for 184 miles between George-town in the District of Columbia and Cumberland in Allegany County, this vestige of the Industrial Revolution and westward U.S. expansion is now one of the mid-Atlantic's most scenic and well-used parks. The Chesapeake and Ohio Canal and adjoining towpath parallel the Potomac River, creating a natural flyway for both water and land birds. Consequently, the C&O Canal is a perennial favorite of bird-ers, with each one swearing that his or her chosen stretch is the best during migration.

Montgomery County's portion of this nar-row but beautiful park runs for a mere 35 miles, from the DC/Maryland line just upstream from Chain Bridge to the Frederick County line at the mouth of the Monocacy River. The canal's "birdy" appeal is enhanced by its relative closeness to centers of population, straightforward auto access, adequate (if sometimes oversubscribed) parking, lack of entry fee (except at Great Falls Park), and hard-packed surface that provides generally easy walking or biking. (Choosing the Billy Goat Trail as an alterna-tive to the towpath along some of the lower stretches of the canal offers a much greater hiking challenge and is recommended only for those in good physical condition and wearing proper footwear.)

With the mighty Potomac alongside and usually visible, the towpath, bordered by a continuous line of trees, can always offer something of interest. If there is a downside to birding here, it is that finding certain

Site at a Glance

C&O Canal

Best birds:
Waterfowl, woodpeckers, vireos/warblers

Habitat:
Riparian woods, open water

Conditions:
Towpath level; occasion-ally muddy and slippery

Best seasons:
Spring and fall

Amenities:
Portable toilets and telephones at some sites. No trash containers in park

habitats—such as grassy or overgrown fields—requires one to move inland out of the park. Also, the towpath can be extremely muddy after rains and slippery following snow and ice. The park is always open except during periods following flood damage, which unfortunately occurs on a regular but unpredictable basis.

This site guide treats the C&O Canal in Montgomery County as a number of separate sections, each of a size suitable for a half day or full day of birding. On some of the longer sections, the use of two cars, one parked at the intended destination, can avoid a hike back to the starting point. A bicycle offers a convenient mode of transportation, particularly on the upper sections beyond Sycamore Landing. A small section of the towpath between Old Angler's Inn and Great Falls requires that bikes be carried briefly over a stony area.

As with all birding, the hours just after dawn and before sunset provide the greatest number and variety of birds, especially in the warmer months. Birding along the towpath in an upstream direction puts the morning sun at one's back.

Although the canal actually runs roughly southeast to northwest, this guide will use "north" or "upstream" to denote movement away from Washington and "south" or "downstream" to indicate the direction towards Washington. Small wooden mile markers, which measure distances from the beginning of the canal in Georgetown at Milepost (MP) 0.0, are on your left as you go upstream—but they can be missed, especially if you're a speedy cyclist. Locations in the text are often given in terms of these distances. (Intermediate mileages, such as MP 27.4, are estimates; do not expect to see wooden stakes at these points!)

Section 1. Chain Bridge (MP 4.2) to Carderock (MP 10.4) —6.2 miles

Access points:

a) **Clara Barton Parkway just north of Chain Bridge.** Parking area beside roadway. Walk up onto north side of bridge and take steps leading down to towpath.

b) **Ridge Road in Brookmont.** From intersection of MacArthur Boulevard and Sangamore Road, take MacArthur 0.2 mile west.

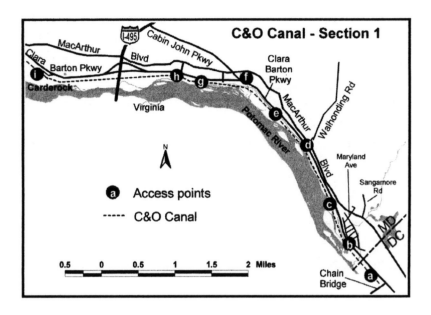

Turn left onto Maryland Avenue and proceed to Ridge Road (one way), then follow Ridge to 61st Street. Park by roadside and take steep path down to pedestrian footbridge over canal to towpath just south of Lock 5 at MP 5.

c) Lock 6, MP 5.4. Clara Barton Parkway, accessible inbound only.* Not accessible 2:30-7:00 p.m. weekdays, when parkway is outbound only. Lot 6 is located just after the parkway widens from two lanes to four. Twelve-space parking lot.

d) MacArthur Boulevard at Walhonding Road, opposite Sycamore Store. Small parking area on MacArthur. Steep path down to footbridge (okay for bikes) and across canal at approximately MP 6.4.

e) Lock 7. Clara Barton Parkway, accessible inbound only.* Eight parking spots. Heavy traffic and noisy but close to lock and towpath at MP 7.0.

f) MacArthur Boulevard, between locks 7 and 8. Small parking lot on west side of MacArthur at south end of single-lane bridge between Glen Echo and Cabin John, just north of Wilson Lane. Trail leads down to steep wooden steps under parkway and across footbridge over canal to towpath.

g) Lock 8. Clara Barton Parkway, accessible inbound only.* Small parking area well off parkway. Long steep path down to canal at MP 8.4.

h) Lock 10. Clara Barton Parkway, accessible inbound only.* Small parking lot by parkway. Quick access to lock and towpath at MP 8.8. Ideal for bike access.

i) Carderock Recreation Area. Take Clara Barton Parkway outbound from I-495 for 0.8 mile, exit at Carderock off-ramp, and follow signs to Carderock. After road goes under canal, turn left at stop sign and park in lot. Or, turn right and make an immediate left into main parking lot. There is another parking lot 0.4 mile farther up road, with a short trail to towpath at MP 10.8.

Traffic outbound from DC can turn around to head inbound at Cabin John or Carderock exits; no turnaround at Glen Echo exit.

Amenities: Excellent restrooms at Carderock parking lots. Public telephone at Carderock. Portable toilet at Lock 8. No food facilities.

Birding notes: The first half-mile of the canal north of Chain Bridge is in the District of Columbia. There is access to the river (still in DC) along a partly paved, cracking road at MP 4.5. The vegetation is low here and inhabited by Song Sparrows and Indigo Buntings. The woods between the canal and the river have breeding Yellow-throated Warblers, and a Mourning Warbler was once found here in late May. Prothonotary Warbler breeds in the wet area just downstream of Chain Bridge and in the wet woods above Fletcher's Boathouse at MP 3.1 (both are DC locations).

The river above Chain Bridge is rocky and is a favored fishing site for people, Great Blue Herons, and Black-crowned Night-Herons. The canal, which is filled with water throughout this section, has numerous Canada Geese and Mallards, with a few Wood Ducks and American Black Ducks. A more exotic duck may turn up once in a while, and Belted Kingfisher makes an occasional appearance. Northern Rough-winged Swallows, which nest in crevices between the stones below Chain Bridge and along the wall below Canal Road downstream in DC, are regular in spring and summer.

The best bet for waterbirds is in the river just below the Little Falls Dam, upstream of Lock 6 at MP 5.5. Herring, Ring-billed, and Great

Black-backed gulls are usually present, but a bigger attraction is the diving ducks—Bufflehead, Common Goldeneye, and Ring-necked in particular—that can be seen on occasion in winter. The slack water above the dam often holds many Common Mergansers in late winter, and Red-breasted Merganser has been spotted here too. Set up your scope beside the big pump house, and after you've scoped the river check the overgrown grass and small trees around you for sparrows and other perching birds.

Bonaparte's Gulls can be seen in good numbers in April, both here and further upstream, and Caspian Terns in late April/early May. Double-crested Cormorants are usually numerous in the rocky sections of the river. About 30 yards south of Lock 11 (MP 9.0), an inconspicuous trail wanders in a generally upstream direction toward the river opposite Plummer's Island, from which Barred Owls can often be heard calling during the day. Working north, you will eventually come to the Beltway Bridge (MP 9.2). This is the Seven Locks stretch, and the elevation rises fairly steeply. Traffic noise makes it almost impossible to hear bird song within a quarter-mile of either side of the bridge. Rock Doves roost under the bridge. Just north of the bridge, Louisiana Waterthrush breeds along the stream that rushes from the canal down to the Potomac.

The rich, moist woods between the canal and river, up to the Carderock parking lots, are home to Acadian Flycatchers and Northern Parulas in summer, and Great Crested Flycatchers and Blue-gray Gnatcatchers are common. In winter, as is true all along the canal, you will meet small flocks of chickadees and titmice, mixed in with Golden-crowned and Ruby-crowned kinglets, Brown Creepers, and the occasional White-breasted Nuthatch. (Red-breasted Nuthatch is rare, due to a dearth of pine trees.) Migrant birds are somewhat easier to see in the trees on the far (east) side of the canal than in the thick woods.

When the water level in the canal is low and mud is exposed, look for Solitary Sandpipers during migration. They can be almost invisible until they fly.

As an alternative to continuing along the towpath to Carderock, look for a blue-blazed trail (part of the Billy Goat Trail) that leads down to the river and then curves upstream to reach the lower

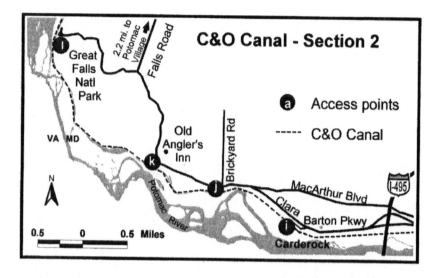

Carderock parking lot. This trail is reached by a short walk toward the river from a point just opposite the remnants of Lock 14 at approximately MP 9.9. The trail can be slippery and has one rocky stream crossing, but early in the day it can afford close views of birds by the river before they are spooked by fishermen. Spotted Sandpiper can be abundant on the rocks and on the riverbank. In winter, look for Common Loon and grebes (Pied-billed or Horned, with the hope of Eared).

Indigo Bunting is particularly common during migration, and orioles of both species can be seen and heard in tall trees along the river. Eastern Kingbirds are everywhere, Northern Parulas are common nesters, and swallows stream by during April and May. If you get here early enough, you may see Common Nighthawks mopping up after a hard night of insect catching.

Section 2. Carderock (MP 10.4) to Great Falls (MP 14.3) —3.9 miles

Access points:

i) **Carderock Recreation Area.** Take Clara Barton Parkway outbound 0.8 mile from I-495, exit at Carderock off-ramp, and follow signs to Carderock. After road goes under canal, turn left at stop sign and park in lot. Or, turn right and make an immediate left into main parking lot. There is another parking lot 0.4 mile farther up road, with a short trail to towpath at MP 10.8.

j) MacArthur Boulevard just north of Brickyard Road. Park carefully, since parking is now prohibited along much of MacArthur Boulevard. From a small gravel area, a footbridge leads to the canal at about MP 11.5.

k) Old Angler's Inn. MacArthur Boulevard 1.1 miles north of the end of Clara Barton Parkway. Two parking lots across from Old Angler's Inn; they fill up quickly on weekends. Service road bridge crosses canal to towpath at MP 12.3.

l) Great Falls National Park (U.S. fee area). Winding, 1.2-mile entrance road (many deer, 15 mph speed limit) begins at intersection of MacArthur Boulevard and Falls Road; this is 1.1 miles north of Old Angler's Inn on MacArthur, or 2 miles south of the intersection of Falls and River Roads in Potomac. Despite extensive parking, all spaces can be filled by noon on busy summer weekends; park is then temporarily closed to additional visitors.

Amenities: Public telephones and excellent restrooms at both Carderock and Great Falls. Great Falls has a small food concession, open daily in summer, 100 yards north of the visitor center in the Great Falls Tavern, which also has a small museum and bookshop. The Old Angler's Inn at Cropley has a delightful but pricey restaurant, best reserved for special occasions such as a 30-warbler-species day on the canal. Potomac Village, at the intersection of River and Falls Roads, has supermarkets, gas stations, pharmacies, and restaurants.

Birding notes: Were it not for the extreme popularity of this stretch of the canal—with canoeists, kayakers, rock climbers, falls watchers, and droves of plain old tourists in summer—this would undoubtedly be the finest birding area close to the Federal City. Some of us think it still may be! If you avoid weekends spring through fall and/or start early in the morning, you will be impressed by the resident and migrant bird life along this four-mile section of the canal and on the adjacent river. At the main picnic area in Carderock, just south of the entrance road, an hour spent birding the trees around the edges of the big lawn during spring migration will pay many dividends. Most of the warblers may be Yellow-rumped, but more than 20 other warbler species have been seen here, including Blue-winged, Golden-winged, Bay-breasted, Magnolia, Chestnut-sided, and Blackburnian. Warbling Vireos and Baltimore Orioles are regulars in the big sycamore trees overhanging the river. Over the river migrate all the eastern swallows, including Bank Swallows and Purple Martins, as well as Chimney Swifts. Watch for them perched on saplings or bushes on small islands in the river. Overhead look for Bald Eagles, Ospreys, Black and Turkey vultures, and Red-tailed and Red-shouldered hawks. In April or September you may see Broad-winged Hawks on the move. Double-crested Cormorants and gulls—look for Bonaparte's in April—coast over the river.

Just above the first restroom area in Carderock, you have a choice of following a small trail to the towpath or cutting down to the river and taking the blue-blazed trail—a relatively easy walk. Downstream lies the area described in Section 1. If you go upstream, you will traverse dry woods where thrushes—mostly Wood Thrush and an occasional Swainson's or Veery—and Ovenbirds should be seen or heard. When you come to a set of rocks favored by apprentice rock-climbers, you can cut back to the northernmost Carderock parking lot and the towpath or continue on the blue-blazed trail until it intersects with the towpath at about MP 11.1. Acadian and Great Crested flycatchers and Eastern Wood-Pewees are common along this section; Least and Yellow-bellied flycatchers have been seen but should not be expected.

Above MP 11, the towpath runs along a high escarpment above the river. You can look at the treetops here for a better view of the birds—Yellow-throated Warbler is regular—or across the canal to a spot where a small stream joins it and Louisiana Waterthrushes can reliably be found in spring and early summer. They are usually on territory by the middle of April. Northern Waterthrush is a migrant only; it is more likely to be found (and heard more often than seen) down towards the river.

At MP 11.5 you will see the wooden footbridge and the trail to MacArthur Boulevard (*access point j*). This, too, is a good area for migrants. One hundred yards upstream from the footbridge is an area where Barred Owls roost and are often seen by day on both sides of the canal. Continuing upstream, the canal broadens considerably. Great Blue and Green herons fish patiently from snags and fallen logs along the far side, and Pileated Woodpeckers can be seen dashing overhead or calling loudly from the woods. (The entire canal is excellent for woodpeckers, but Pileateds are distinctly more common from Great Falls downstream to Chain Bridge than they are farther up the river.)

Just past the Barred Owl area, look for the beginning of the Billy Goat Trail descending into the woods on your left. This branch of the blue-blazed trail runs for 1.4 miles through the woods and eventually rejoins the towpath. It is moderately demanding, especially when conditions are wet and the river is high, as a number of rocky areas may have to be climbed. But the surroundings are magnificent and you have an opportunity to sit on a rock by the river, catch your breath, and scan the waters and the skies. If you elect to stay on the towpath and work your way upstream, you will notice a marshy pond on the far side of the canal at around MP 12. Prothonotary Warbler may be seen and heard here in the summer.

At Old Angler's Inn (*access point k*), numerous kayakers and canoeists can be seen carrying their craft down to a calm put-in point by the river. This area is almost always a hive of human activity; move through with all deliberate speed. The towpath was totally destroyed here in the 1996 flood but has been beautifully reconstructed and the canal rewatered.

Just north of the small parking lot nearest the canal, reached by a steep set of steps, is the beginning of the Berm (or "Berma") Road, which you can use as an alternative to the towpath as a route toward Great Falls. It runs through deep woods and can be superb for warblers and vireos during migration. Philadelphia Vireo was found here in the spring of 1999. The Berm Road connects back to the towpath via a small bridge (you'll have to carry your bike briefly) at about MP 13.8.

If you elect to follow the towpath northwards to Great Falls, you will quickly come upon Widewater, where the Canal was constructed over an ancient channel of the Potomac. The water here is very deep as well as wide, but it does not seem to attract many birds apart from Great Blue Heron. As you proceed north, you will notice that the vegetation on the berm (right) side is dominated by smaller

Philadelphia Vireo

trees such as arborvitae. This is not a particularly birdy area, but the landscape is astonishingly lovely and views skyward are unimpeded, so watch for raptors and swallows. Resist the temptation to detour on the Billy Goat Trail where you see the sign at about MP 12.7; this trail can best be described as "rugged" and is not recommended for birders.

A little farther upstream, the towpath deteriorates into a narrow path, then to a rocky jumble. You will have to heft your bike for 20–30 yards if you are cycling. Soon though, the regular, smooth towpath resumes at the Six Locks area. In winter, berry-loving birds such as American Robins and Cedar Waxwings are found here. This is also one of many good places along the canal to catch a glimpse of Winter Wren in the colder months. Unfortunately, this skulker does not start singing its ethereal song until shortly before moving north in April.

At MP 13.8 you will see the northern terminus of the Billy Goat Trail. Just downstream, the wooden footbridge linking the towpath to the Berm Road crosses the canal. Between this point and Great

Falls Tavern, 0.5 mile ahead, the elevation rises steeply. To your left at MP 14.1, just above Lock 17, you will see a very popular trail leading to the edge of the Falls; you wouldn't believe how many people use this trail spring through fall. It is not usually notable for birds, but you should not miss the view of the river in flood from this vantage point.

The best birding in the vicinity of Great Falls is north of the tavern (visitor center) and is described in Section 3.

Section 3. Great Falls (MP 14.3) to Pennyfield Lock (MP 19.6)—5.3 miles

Access points:

l) Great Falls National Park (U.S. fee area). Winding, 1.2-mile entrance road (many deer, 15 mph speed limit) begins at intersection of MacArthur and Falls Road; this is 1.1 miles north of Old Angler's Inn on MacArthur, or 2 miles south of the intersection of Falls and River Roads in Potomac. Despite extensive parking lots, all spaces can be filled by noon on busy summer weekends; park is then temporarily closed to additional visitors.

m) Swain's Lock. Off River Road, 2.2 miles northwest of Potomac Village. One-half mile beyond traffic light at Piney Meetinghouse Road, turn left on Swain's Lock Road (signs are inconspicuous). Very small parking lot at end of road.

n) Pennyfield Lock. Off River Road, 5.3 miles northwest of Potomac Village. Just 0.1 mile beyond Travilah Road, you will see Pennyfield Lock Road on your left (and Esworthy Road on your right). Be careful turning left—the hill makes it difficult to see oncoming River Road traffic. At 0.6 mile, you will cross a small bridge and see the canal in front of you; turn left and continue for another 0.4 mile to a small parking lot at the very end of the road. Park and walk a short distance in the same (downstream) direction, and cross to towpath at lock.

Amenities: Public telephones and excellent restrooms at Great Falls. Great Falls has a small food concession, open daily in summer, and a small museum in the Great Falls Tavern (visitor center). Swain's Lock has a small concession shop, open March to November, with ice cream and cold drinks, as well as canoe and bicycle rentals. Pennyfield has a single portable toilet, which is usually in usable

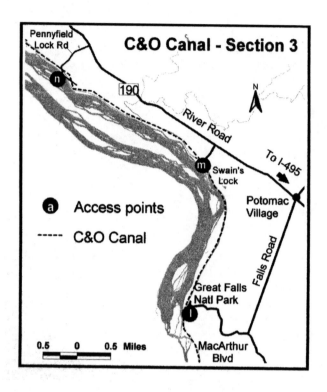

condition. Swain's has a large, attractive and shaded picnic area with many tables, but it is popular with groups and can be very busy. Potomac Village, at the intersection of River and Falls Roads, has supermarkets, gas stations, pharmacies, and restaurants.

Birding notes: Arrive at Great Falls Park at dawn on a May morning and you will be rewarded by a large variety of local and migrant birds, led probably by orioles and tanagers in the trees around the visitor center and parking areas, as well as warblers and vireos. The open skies above hold both vulture species and are worth watching for hawks in season—Red-tailed and Red-shouldered are regular, and American Kestrels are around during migration.

In winter you will want to head across the lock (Lock 20) by the Tavern and just upstream to the broad platform that overlooks the slack river water backed up by the dam. Ducks and geese float nonchalantly, apparently oblivious to the chaotic torrents just downstream. Canada Geese and Mallards are the most conspicuous birds, but American Black Duck, American Wigeon, Wood Ducks, Ring-necked Ducks, Buffleheads, Common and Hooded mergansers, and Lesser Scaup are also regular in winter, with Redheads an occasional delightful surprise. Such locally uncommon birds as Long-tailed Duck, Red-throated Loon, and Red-necked Phalarope have been seen from this spot, usually during migration periods. With your scope in the southernmost position on the platform, by the rail, you can look upstream at the Bald Eagle nest on the island in the river. This is the closest active eagle nest to the nation's capital. (See the Little Treasures section of the guide for a fuller description of this fascinating place.) Outside the nesting season (February–April), the eagles are often seen well away from the nest area.

Waterfowl on the river in winter are best seen by quietly walking the riverside trail that leaves the towpath just north of the platform, at about MP 14.4. This trail runs for more than a mile along the edge of the river, eventually looping back to join the towpath at MP 15.8, just below the City of Rockville water intake pump-house. It is an easy walk (except during periods of high water or recent rains) and allows close views of wintering waterfowl (an immature Surf Scoter was here one memorable May Count day), Winter Wren, Hermit Thrush, woodpeckers, and possible Barred Owl.

The towpath from Great Falls (MP 14.4) to Swain's Lock (MP 16.7) is notable for the large number of breeding Prothonotary Warblers and Acadian Flycatchers. All of the regularly occurring migrant warblers have been seen in this stretch, including Blackburnian, Bay-breasted, and Cerulean. The woods on the far side of the canal are drier, and the perceptive birder can hear (although probably not see) Wood Thrush, Red-eyed Vireo, and Scarlet Tanager at frequent intervals throughout the summer.

MP 16. 7 brings you to Swain's Lock (*access point m*), an area popular with school groups and fishermen. Check out the picnic area down by the river for Warbling Vireo in summer and woodpeckers in the cooler months.

Above Swain's, at MP 17.4, you come upon the WSSC's water extraction area, which feeds the filtration plant to the east on River Road.

Trees are smaller here, and there is a pipeline cut just upstream; bird species differ from those in the adjacent heavily wooded areas at all seasons. In winter, Song Sparrows are common (watch for Field Sparrows in summer), while singing Indigo Buntings are everywhere starting in late April; listen too for possible Prairie Warbler. Look over the wall below the WSSC structures, where a channel of the river runs directly under your view. With luck, you may see herons or kingfishers fishing or ducks moving in for easy feeding in the slow-moving waters. Upstream, the vegetation becomes larger again, but the river is soon in clear view above MP 18.0. A small but growing Great Blue Heron colony can be seen in large trees over on the Virginia shoreline (Fairfax County) at around MP 18.5.

The rest of the way to Pennyfield Lock (MP 19.6) the river is constantly in view and should be checked for waterfowl at all times of the year. This stretch is most easily reached by going to Pennyfield Lock and working downstream. Over on the canal side, the trees hold a wide variety of resident perching birds and many migrant warblers, vireos, and flycatchers. All the common woodpeckers, including Northern Flickers in migration and winter and Yellow-bellied Sapsuckers in winter, should be spotted without great difficulty. Listen for the gentle song of Brown Creeper in early spring.

Section 4: Pennyfield Lock (MP 19.6) to Seneca/Riley's Lock (MP 22.8)—3.2 miles

Access points:

n) **Pennyfield Lock.** Off River Road, 5.3 miles northwest of Potomac Village. Just 0.1 mile beyond Travilah Road, you will see Pennyfield Lock Road on your left (and Esworthy Road on your right). Be careful turning left—the hill makes it difficult to see oncoming River Road traffic. At 0.6 mile, you will cross a small bridge and see the canal in front of you; turn left and continue for another 0.4 mile to a small parking lot at the very end of the road. Park and walk a short distance in the same (downstream) direction, and cross to towpath at lock.

o) **Violette's Lock.** Off River Road, 7.9 miles northwest of Potomac Village. At 2.6 miles past Pennyfield Lock Road, turn left at Violette's Lock Road. This is a sharp left turn in the middle of a big right-hand

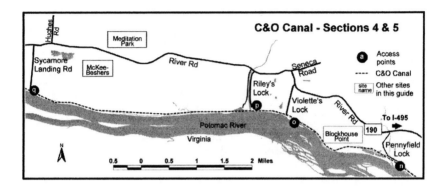

bend in the road less than 0.3 mile past Manor Stone Drive on right. Go 0.6 mile to parking lot at lock.

p) Seneca/Riley's Lock. Off River Road, 8.9 northwest of Potomac Village. Drive 0.2 mile beyond Violette's Lock Road to a T-junction and stop sign. Here River Road makes a left turn and is joined by Seneca Road (Route 112) from the right. Turn left, go 0.8 mile, and turn left onto Riley's Lock Road, continuing 0.7 mile to large parking lot below old lock house.

Amenities: All three access points have portable toilets. Pennyfield and Violette's have just one each, but Seneca now has four spiffy new ones! Poole's General Store, on the north side of River Road just beyond Riley's Lock Road, sells a variety of supplies and basic foods and is open most of the year. Other stores and restaurants, including McDonald's, are 6–7 miles away in Poolesville.

Birding notes: This area is a perennial favorite of local birders, particularly from mid-April to mid-May, when you can observe first-hand just how much birding as a hobby has increased in popularity. The birding is excellent before you even leave the parking area: a Mourning Warbler was found one year in May, and a Philadelphia Vireo was the first bird found on a trip in late September.

Look and listen carefully as you cross the lock and move slowly upstream toward Blockhouse Point (MP 21 and above). The woods between the canal and the river abut channels of the Potomac and harbor breeding Prothonotary Warblers and Louisiana Waterthrushes. A relatively easy path enters this area beside the old lock house, but beware the stinging nettles! Northern Waterthrush sings his loud, distinctive song during spring migration. Acadian Flycatchers call, daring you to spot their almost motionless forms. The big trees above you hold warblers and vireos during migration; more than 20 species of warblers and all six vireo species have been spotted here.

Upstream a bit, around MP 20, you will see the Dierssen Wildlife Area on your left. This area was formerly a good deal wetter than it has been in recent years, and it has become quite overgrown. Watch for Swamp, Song and White-throated (winter) sparrows and Common Yellowthroat. Indigo Buntings sing in the trees around the edge of the area, while Solitary Sandpipers are regular migrants here and in the impoundment a half-mile further upstream. Their camouflage is so effective that they can be practically invisible until they move. You can walk around the first area on a short trail that loops back to the towpath in little more than a quarter-mile. Just beware of ticks, nettles, and poison ivy—as annoying here as anywhere along the C&O Canal. Warbling Vireos have nested in the big sycamore trees. You should also check for Spotted Sandpipers (common) and swallows down along the river.

The next section of towpath upstream from this area is bordered on the west by an extensive wet area. Depending on the amount of water present, you should look in this impoundment for ducks (Wood Ducks, Blue-winged Teal, and Hooded Merganser are the most likely in breeding season, but Gadwall and Green-winged Teal have also been seen), herons (Yellow-crowned Night-Heron is occasional) and Yellow and Prothonotary warblers. Large flocks of Great Egrets may stop here in late summer.

Still further upstream there is a pipeline cut at about MP 20.8; Cerulean Warblers, Black-throated Green Warblers, and Yellow-throated Vireos have been spotted regularly in the vicinity. If you protect yourself from mud and ticks, you can make the short trek down to the river along the cut. It is possible to take a *very* rough path along the river back downstream to the first Dierssen impoundment. This path is good for warblers (including a Golden-winged in fall 1998). The trees by the river may have migrants—in May 1999 numerous Chestnut-sided Warblers were found here.

The woods on the left as you work your way along the towpath from the pipeline cut up to Blockhouse Point are usually very wet and hold breeding Wood Ducks. On the right, dead trees may have woodpeckers—Red-headed is possible—and/or flycatchers (hope for an Olive-sided in fall migration). This section has occasionally had Summer Tanager during migration, a quite uncommon species this far north and west on the Piedmont. Listen too for the distinctive trill of Worm-eating Warbler in the steep, dry woods on the far side of the canal; they probably nest here.

Above MP 21 you become very aware of the river on your left: a rough torrent with many channels, turbulent in all but the driest periods. In winter, diving ducks, especially Buffleheads and Common Mergansers, work the rapids or rest on the rocks. In migration, you never know what might turn up—one June a Sanderling was seen on the rocks. Spotted Sandpiper and Double-crested Cormorants are common in spring and summer, the latter also through fall. There is a wonderful view of the broad river at this spot, and a spotting scope is very helpful. In May 1997, some fortunate (and skillful) MCC birders saw a Scissor-tailed Flycatcher hawking insects off the mid-stream rocks.

Blockhouse Point—a beautiful area where delicately foliaged and cedar-topped cliffs jut into the canal—is more quickly reached from Violette's Lock (*access point o*), about a mile upstream. Be on the lookout for roosting Black Vultures, which breed hereabouts. In the spring, this stretch is a riot of wildflowers, and in migration it can attract colorful mixes of buntings, orioles, tanagers, and grosbeaks. It is also home to nesting Northern Parulas, Yellow-throated Warblers, and Louisiana Waterthrushes.

The parking lot at Violette's Lock can be good for roosting Common Nighthawks in May. They sit on the branches of the medium-sized trees and can be quite difficult to pick out. Behind the parking lot, Louisiana Waterthrushes call in early spring. The parking lot edges have proven to be a real hotspot in spring migration, with tanagers, orioles, and cuckoos in numbers, plus a wide variety of warblers, including Blue-winged, Black-and-white, Brewster's (hybrid), Canada, Wilson's, and American Redstart.

Water for the canal is admitted at Violette's Lock, and above this point the canal is generally dry. Keep an eye out for birds in the small trees and shrubs in the canal bed as you walk upstream. You will soon come to a grassy area that opens onto the river; this is a good place to look out over the water. Moreover, the high trees surrounding this patch have held warblers, vireos, and flycatchers. The creek that runs along the downstream border of this area should also be checked; the edges have yielded a variety of warblers, including Magnolia, Canada, and Mourning. The rest of the stretch between Violette's and Seneca can be fairly quiet, becoming birdy again as you approach Riley's Lock.

Section 5. Seneca/Riley's Lock (MP 22.8) to Sycamore Landing (MP 27.2)—4.4 miles

Access points:

p) **Seneca/Riley's Lock.** Off River Road, 8.9 northwest of Potomac Village. Drive 0.2 mile beyond Violette's Lock Road to a T-junction and stop sign. Here River Road makes a left turn and is joined by Seneca Road (Route 112) from the right. Turn left, go 0.8 mile, and turn left onto Riley's Lock Road, continuing 0.7 mile to large parking lot below old lock house.

q) **Sycamore Landing.** Off River Road, 13.0 miles northwest of Potomac Village. Drive 4.1 miles beyond Riley's Lock Road to Sycamore Landing Road. Turn left and proceed 0.8 mile to parking lot adjacent to canal at very end of road.

Amenities: Seneca has new portable toilets at the rear of the parking lot. Poole's General Store, on the north side of River Road just beyond Riley's Lock Road, sells a variety of supplies and basic foods. Other stores and restaurants, including McDonald's, are 6–7 miles away in Poolesville.

Birding notes: This section of the canal, at least the first 1.5 miles north of Seneca, is almost as popular with birders as the Pennyfield Lock stretch. The Potomac at this point is a broad, slow-moving lake, unfortunately much beloved of operators of fast and noisy watercraft. Set up your scope on the walkway atop the aqueduct right by the old lock house. In winter and early spring, check the river for waterfowl: Common Loon, Pied-billed and Horned grebes

(Red-necked Grebe in 1994 and 1996), Tundra Swan, and miscellaneous diving and puddle ducks—Common and Red-breasted mergansers, Ruddy Duck, Ring-necked Duck, Lesser Scaup, Gadwall, and American Wigeon. Check gulls for Bonaparte's Gull or terns. Cliff Swallows started to nest under the aqueduct a few years ago. This species is otherwise difficult to find in the county (except at Brighton Dam) outside of migration. Eastern Phoebe also likes to nest on the aqueduct; in 1999 one pair placed its nest on a sheltered shelf on the upstream side.

Just north of the aqueduct, a path curves inland south of the small pond (once a boat basin). In the woods alongside, Barred and Great Horned owls are regularly seen and probably nest. Red-headed Woodpecker is occasionally seen in this area; formerly this flashy species was more common than it is now, although sightings have recently increased. Where the path comes to the ruins of a stone-cutting mill, listen for Acadian Flycatcher and Louisiana Waterthrush. The pond always has one or two pairs of Prothonotary Warblers and nesting Wood Ducks and Hooded Mergansers (the latter not every year). Be sure to check this body of water at all times of year, to see what might have arrived unexpectedly.

Upstream, beyond MP 23, the canal becomes swampy and overgrown and should be checked thoroughly for resident and migrant birds. Green Herons are regular. Further again upstream, where the canal backs to a high, rocky bank, the area can be wonderful for warblers, including Yellow-throated. Then the canal dries out, with sizable trees growing in its bed. Still farther north, the towpath passes below a shadowy canopy of trees, a wonderful area to hike or bike during the hot, humid, sunny days of summer. Several Cerulean Warblers were heard singing around MP 25.5 in mid-June 1999 (probable breeders). Ceruleans are known to favor box elder trees, which are present here, for nesting.

At MP 26 is the Horse Pen Branch hiker-biker overnight camp location, with its hand-cranked water pump and just-about-acceptable toilet. Across the canal bed, a narrow trail leads eventually to the Hughes Hollow area (see McKee-Beshers site description). This entire area is terrific for resident and migrant birds. Expect to find all the resident woodpeckers, including (with luck!) Red-headed, augmented by Yellow-breasted Sapsucker in winter. Gray Catbirds are abundant in summer and White-throated Sparrows in winter. Wet and muddy parts of the canal bed are attractive to Rusty Blackbird over the winter months; watch carefully for them, quietly picking over leaves in search for food. Kentucky Warbler can often be heard in spring, and perhaps breeds in wet woods between Horse Pen Branch and Sycamore Landing. As you approach MP 27 in the spring, listen for Cerulean Warblers singing vociferously.

Section 6. Sycamore Landing (MP 27.2) to Edward's Ferry (MP 30.8)—3.6 miles

Access points:

q) Sycamore Landing. Off River Road, 13.0 miles northwest of Potomac Village. Drive 4.1 miles beyond Riley's Lock Road to Sycamore Landing Road. Turn left and proceed 0.8 mile to parking lot adjacent to canal at very end of road.

r) Edward's Ferry. From Poolesville, take Willard Road south 0.6 mile, turn right on Westerly Road, and continue 1.4 miles to intersection with Edward's Ferry Road. Turn left and proceed 2.5 miles to end of Edward's Ferry Road, cross at lock, and park in small lot by canal. Lot may be crowded with boat trailers in summer.

Amenities: No food services or restrooms in this section. Boat ramp at Edward's Ferry.

Birding notes: This is a wonderful birding area, though few birders use it. Winter Wren is almost a sure thing in the canal bed near the path leading from the Sycamore Landing parking lot to the towpath. Look for Hairy Woodpeckers and Yellow-bellied Sapsuckers (winter) in the trees between the towpath and the river. Birding trips have sometimes seen Barred Owls during the day; they nest and roost in the large sycamores along the river.

Northeast from MP 28 lies the Summit Hall Turf Farm, formerly an accessible birding location noted for "grasspipers" in fall and American Pipits in winter, but now out of bounds as a result of thoughtless and irresponsible behavior by some birders. It still may be possible to set up a scope on the towpath and look east over the large expanse of manicured turf, hoping for a Buff-breasted Sandpiper or American Golden-Plover in August or September, Horned Lark in November, or American Pipit in January. In any

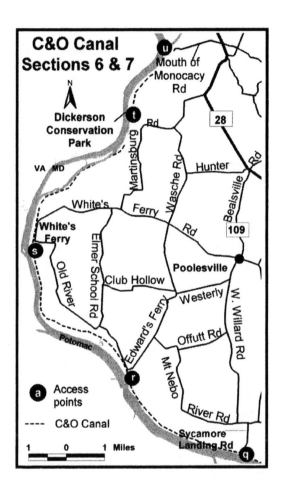

event, birders should keep a weather eye out for sandpipers and smaller birds when walking the towpath in this vicinity. At the very least, Killdeer should be seen and heard. In wet weather, pools of water that form in parts of the Turf Farm may attract ducks and geese in winter or Solitary and other sandpipers during migration. American Kestrels quarter this area, too. Red-shouldered Hawks nest nearby and are often seen and heard.

Above MP 29 one loses sight of the turf farm on the right and the river disappears to the left. The next mile is an excellent birding area, as trees arch over the towpath, blocking the sun. The canal bed is overgrown by weeds and small trees, and the wetter areas host Louisiana Waterthrushes, Prothonotary Warblers, and Northern Waterthrushes (in migration). Look for Canada Warbler during migration in areas of low saplings. The best birding areas in this stretch are more easily and quickly reached by working south from Edwards Ferry.

Section 7. Edward's Ferry (MP 30.8) via White's Ferry and Dickerson to Monocacy Aqueduct (MP 42.2)—11.4 miles
Access points:

r) Edward's Ferry. From Poolesville, take Willard Road south 0.6 mile, turn right on Westerly Road, and continue 1.4 miles to intersection with Edward's Ferry Road. Turn left and proceed 2.5 miles to end of Edward's Ferry Road, cross at lock, and park in small lot by canal. Lot may be crowded with boat trailers in summer.

s) White's Ferry. From Poolesville, proceed west on White's Ferry Road 6.3 miles to White's Ferry. Park in large lot on right side of road, avoiding traffic waiting for ferry to Virginia. Access to towpath is a little behind you.

Alternatively, drive north on "old" River Road (gravel surface and occasionally bumpy) 5.3 miles from Edward's Ferry, or 10.4 miles from Sycamore Landing Road. See directions for "Back Roads" in Little Treasures.

t) Dickerson Conservation Park. From Poolesville, take White's Ferry Road west 3.5 miles to Martinsburg Road. Turn right and proceed 2.5 miles to park sign on left. Parking lot is 0.9 mile down road, just short of canal.

Alternatively, from I-270, take exit 6B, Route 28, west about 18 miles, through Darnestown and Beallsville. Some 2.2 miles past Beallsville Road (Route 109), Route 28 makes a sharp right turn (yellow blinking light) and Martinsburg Road goes off to the left. Turn—cautiously—onto Martinsburg Rd. In about 2 miles you will see the park sign on right. Proceed as above.

u) Monocacy Aqueduct. From I-270, take exit 6B, Route 28, west through Darnestown and Beallsville to the small town of Dickerson. After passing the stop sign at Mount Ephraim Road, drive 0.3 mile and turn left on Mouth of Monocacy Road. Proceed 1.4 miles, keeping left at fork, to parking lot just south of handsome aqueduct over Monocacy River, the dividing line between Montgomery and Frederick counties.

Amenities: Small store and outside public telephone at White's Ferry; store open from April to October, generally from 10 a.m. to 7 p.m. weekdays, with longer hours on weekends. Store also rents canoes. Many picnic tables down by the ferry landing—technically for store patrons only, so buy something there if you want to picnic. Substantial toilets/washrooms (summer only) and two portable toilets in the parking lot at White's Ferry and two at Monocacy Aqueduct. Just one picnic table in Dickerson Conservation Park. There is also a very clean portable toilet in the Marble Quarry campsite at MP 38.2. Poolesville, 6 miles away, has fast food, groceries, and several gas stations.

Birding: Few Montgomery birders regularly work the canal in these "northern" parts, particularly the Edward's Ferry (MP 30.8) to Dickerson Conservation Park (MP 40) stretch, where the access points are a long way apart, far from a main road, and tricky to find without good directions or a map. Yet there are many advantages in doing so. Travelers are few and far between, even in the busy spring and summer months. The scenery is gorgeous and the birds much the same as those at the more popular birding stretches to the south. A bicycle is the ideal way to explore these parts.

The river is never far away in this section, though sometimes out of direct view, and should be checked for ducks, loons, and grebes in the cooler months. Warblers, vireos, and flycatchers can be numerous during migration. The only disadvantage of these happy facts is that you are unlikely to run across a fellow birder to assist with an ID unless you take a birding buddy along with you.

The canal bed is generally overgrown with small trees, bushes, and/or weeds in this section (apart from a two-mile stretch above Dickerson, which is watered). Alder Flycatcher has been found (in migration only) in swampier areas along this stretch, together with the nesting Acadian and occasional Least flycatcher in the woods. Warbling and Yellow-throated vireos are regular in the more extensively wooded stretches, together with the more common Red-eyed

Northern Bobwhite

Vireo, a customary breeder. Louisiana and Northern waterthrushes (the latter migrant only) frequent the streams and swampy areas, respectively. Prothonotary Warbler nests in wetter areas, and in the woods there are American Redstart and Black-and-white Warbler. Barred and Great Horned owls are quite common, and may be seen occasionally in the daylight hours.

The fields inland from Edward's Ferry and White's Ferry are worth visiting in March and April for displaying American Woodcock after dusk. Northern Bobwhite is a rare species these days in Montgomery County, but one was heard calling from fields close to the towpath near MP 32 in June 1999.

White's Ferry (MP 35.5) is an interesting, if busy, place to stop for a snack or breather. It also offers an easy opportunity to do some birding in the Lucketts area of Loudoun County, VA. Drive onto the "General Jubal Early" for a quick and inexpensive ferry crossing.

Back on the towpath and above White's Ferry, starting just before MP 37, there is a slow-moving side channel of the river just to your left that looks like a medium-sized pond; watch for Great Blue and Green herons. An adult Bald Eagle was seen fishing here in July 1999. At MP 39.2 a historical marker tells you that White's Ford used to be nearby—Confederate forces used it several times to cross the river during the Civil War—but the modern traveler can see no trace of it.

Dickerson Conservation Park (MP 39.6), just a little further along, is an interesting and (hallelujah!) unimproved area. The overgrown fields on either side of the access road to the parking lot from Martinsburg Road harbor Prairie Warbler and Yellow-breasted Chat in summer and sparrows in winter. Red-shouldered Hawks nest nearby and have been seen and heard at all times of the year. The canal upstream from this little park is watered almost all the way to Lock 27 at MP 41.5, and this is a good stretch to look for Belted Kingfisher and assorted woodpeckers in the many dead trees. This stretch is also quite open (and hot in summer) and there are White-eyed Vireos and Eastern Towhees in the low bushes.

Just before you come upon the warm-water discharge from the power plant at about MP 40.5 (and the fascinating white-water slalom course PEPCO engineers built for Olympic kayakers), there is a swampy area in the canal that can hold Green Heron and both waterthrushes. In these open areas, Barn and Northern Rough-winged swallows swoop for insects, and you have a chance to look up for hawks and vultures—and maybe an eagle. The more wooded and shady parts of the towpath have a remarkably large number of Acadian Flycatchers in spring and summer, while the sunnier areas abound with the song of Indigo Buntings. An Acadian Flycatcher nest with young was found overhanging the towpath at MP 38.5 in summer 1999. Warbling Vireos obligingly warble in large trees, particularly sycamores, along the riverbank. Look for Rusty Blackbird from November through April in wet and muddy areas of the canal. Downstream of the PEPCO plant in colder winters, look for water-fowl taking advantage of the warm-water discharge from the plant's electricity generators. Note, however, that it is not always easy to get a close view of the river unless you are much farther downstream than the kayak course. If you leave the towpath, beware of poison ivy, stinging nettles, ticks, and unpredictable holes in the ground. Upstream of the power plant, the river is clearly visible on your left and there is a steep rock cliff on your right; the view is unbeatable. Just after you pass MP 42 you will see the Monocacy Aqueduct—still awaiting a thorough refurbishing. Beyond it lies Frederick County, with its own set of ornithological challenges and opportunities! Ƴ

— *Mike Bowen*

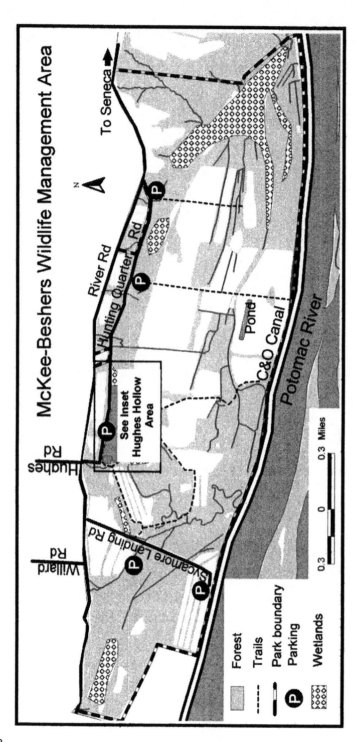

McKee-Beshers Wildlife Management Area

To Seneca

N

River Rd

Hunting Quarter Rd

P

P

See Inset
Hughes Hollow
Area

Hughes Rd

Willard Rd

Sycamore Landing Rd

P

P

Pond

C&O Canal

Potomac River

0.3   0   0.3   Miles

Forest
Trails
Park boundary
Parking
Wetlands

P

McKee-Beshers WMA, Poolesville

Situated mostly on the rich floodplain of the Potomac River, McKee-Beshers WMA (which includes the area known to birders as Hughes Hollow) offers a mosaic of habitats over its almost 2,000 acres—forest, crop fields, overgrown fields, wooded swamps, large hedgerows, and marshes. In 30 years of birding the area, I have recorded more than 230 species, including about 70 that nest there annually. Birding can be a rewarding experience at any time of year, although the best time is probably October–May, when mosquitoes and deer flies are scarce. Since the area is often wet and muddy, it is best to wear rubber boots when visiting. The area is largely undeveloped with only a few clearly marked trails, but by following the maintenance roads and mowed paths around the wood-field edges and through the fields, you can cover a large portion of it.

It is important to keep in mind that McKee-Beshers is a public hunting area. Hunting occurs primarily from September through

Site at a Glance

McKee-Beshers

Best birds:
Waterfowl, woodpeckers, thrushes/forest species, vireos/warblers, sparrows

Habitat:
Fields (mowed and overgrown), woods, hedgerows, swamps

Conditions:
Level; often wet/muddy; buggy; hunting in season

Best seasons:
Year-round

Amenities:
None

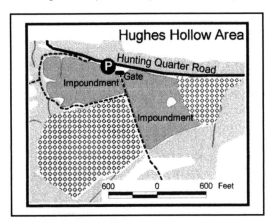

Hughes Hollow Area

600   0   600 Feet

December, and to a lesser extent from January until mid-February and from mid-April to mid-May. If you are familiar with the hunting seasons and regulations, you can coexist with hunters while birding. My experience has been that within a week or so after the start of a hunting season the number of hunters greatly diminishes. The only exception to this rule—and the only time I would not bird there—is the last week of November and the first week of December, during firearm deer season. Birders who would rather not deal with hunters will find Sunday the ideal day to visit, since hunting is not permitted then.

Directions: From I-495, take exit 39, River Road (Route 190), toward Potomac. Drive west for 11.4 miles (going through Potomac Village) to a T-intersection and stop sign. Here River Road turns to the left and is joined by Seneca Road (Route 112) from the right. Turn left at the stop sign and drive west on River Road. In 2.0 miles you will see a large sign on the left marking the eastern boundary of McKee-Beshers. Continue another 2.5 miles to Hughes Road. Turn left, and follow the road—which shortly makes a left turn—to a parking area on the right.

From I-270, take exit 6B, Route 28, toward Darnestown, and drive west 7.5 miles to Seneca Road (Route 112) (a traffic light). Turn left. In 2.8 miles, Seneca Road will become River Road. Continue as above.

Suggested routes: After parking, walk around the metal gate and go straight ahead onto the large dike. There are three visible impound-ments: a large one to the left and two smaller ones, separated by another dike, to the right. This impoundment/dike area is referred to as Hughes Hollow by local birders. The impoundments to the right and left have similar dense aquatic vegetation (mainly bullhead lilies) during the growing season and open water at other times. The second impoundment on your right is a buttonbush swamp inter-spersed with willows.

The main dike is a good spot for viewing a wide variety of water and land birds. During early spring, scan the water for Pied-billed Grebes, Blue- and Green-winged teal, Ring-necked and Wood ducks, and Hooded Mergansers. Later in the spring, look for Sora, Virginia Rail, and Common Moorhen among the aquatic vegetation. I have twice seen Purple Gallinules in the large impoundment to the left.

During migration, look for warblers in the willows that border the dike on your right. Least Bitterns, Willow Flycatchers, Yellow and Prothonotary warblers, Orchard Orioles, and Red-winged Blackbirds nest in this area. Eastern Bluebirds and Tree Swallows often use the cavities in the willows excavated earlier by woodpeckers. Later in the summer, depending on water levels, Great Blue Herons, Great Egrets, Green Herons, and occasionally Little Blue Herons start congregating in the large impoundment. Fall brings Rusty Blackbirds and a variety of sparrows, including Swamp Sparrows. At any time of the year, listen for Red-shouldered Hawks and Barred Owls calling. In fall and winter, look for Winter Wrens and listen for Red-headed Woodpeckers in the woods bordering the southern edge of the impoundments. Unfortunately, due to silting and the growth of aquatic vegetation, Hughes Hollow no longer provides good habitat for shorebirds.

Continue birding southeast along the main dike and pass through a wooded area. Just past the tree line you will come to an open area with fields on both sides. Turn right and walk west, following a path through the field (an evergreen stand will be on your left and the tree line on your right). The deciduous trees can be good in migration for vireos and warblers. This is a good place to look for Red-headed Woodpecker, and the tops of the pines often hold singing Indigo Buntings. After you have birded this area, return to the main dike, then retrace your steps until you reach the cross-dike, now to your left. Follow this dike and loop around the impoundment toward Hunting Quarter Road, keeping an eye out on the left for an occasional American Bittern. Eventually, as you begin to turn right, the area becomes more wooded and is a good place to look for landbird migrants. As you near the end of the trail, you will see a set of steps on your left leading up to the road. South of these steps, there is a somewhat overgrown path between a very small fourth impoundment and the one you just circled. Often this path is not accessible because of high water, but if it is dry you can follow it to gain a different view of the impoundment. Return to the steps, ascend to the road, and turn right to return to the parking lot.

If conditions warrant, once back at the parking lot you can walk along the northern edge of the larger impoundment on Hunting Quarter Road until you reach the wooded swamp. I often do this to

Eastern Phoebe

get better views of birds such as Wood Duck and Hooded Merganser that are hard to see from the dike.

Once back in your car, drive east along Hunting Quarter Road (unpaved, sometimes muddy and filled with potholes, but passable except after a very heavy rain) about 0.8 mile until you reach another parking lot. The road beyond the metal gate eventually leads to the Potomac River. Park and take this road bordered by swampy woods (often a good place during migration for Wood Ducks and Rusty Blackbirds), crossing a culvert. Just beyond the swampy woods you will reach a large stretch of fields divided by tall hedgerows. Originally planted as rows of autumn olive, bush honeysuckle, and other species, these hedgerows have grown into small stands of trees where such species as Wood Thrush and Gray Catbird (probably the most abundant breeding species in the area) nest. In fall and winter, Cedar Waxwing, American Robin, Hermit Thrush, and Purple Finch feed on the abundant berries. During spring and summer, look for a variety of field birds, including Common Yellowthroat, Field and Song sparrows, Indigo Bunting, American Goldfinch, and an occasional Blue Grosbeak.

About 175 yards beyond the swampy woods, there is usually a cultivated strip of sunflowers, millet, and other food plants. Although planted mainly for Mourning Doves and Northern Bobwhite, it also attracts sparrows in fall and winter. I have seen American Tree, Vesper, Fox, Song, Swamp, White-throated, and White-crowned sparrows and Dark-eyed Juncos here. Several of these food strips with varying crops are planted every year throughout McKee-Beshers, but this is one of the easiest to find.

As you continue walking, you will pass several more fields and a stand of trees with an old concrete water trough on your right. About 0.25 mile past the trough you will come to a second swampy woods with a second culvert beneath the road and with a readily noticeable concrete structure on the right side of the road. You will soon reach a narrow strip of swampy woodland with another group of fields beyond. Look to your right for a grassy strip that is sometimes mowed. Turn right and walk down the strip; the woods are now on your right and the overgrown field is on your left. Look on your left for a series of small ponds that extend almost to the stand of trees in the distance. Depending on water levels, there may be herons, ducks, or shorebirds here. Return to the main road and resume your walk towards the river. On the other side of the next hedgerow is a larger pond on your right, the only one clearly visible from the road. During dry periods, this pond may be the major source of drinking water for local birds.

If you are not ready to return to the parking lot after checking these ponds, you can continue walking down the road and then through the woods to the C&O Canal. The road will intersect the canal about 0.3 mile southeast of the Horse Pen hiker-biker overnight camp location at MP 26. Note that you must cross the canal (can be dry or wet) to reach the towpath, and on your return it may be difficult to find the place where you first emerged.

Return to your car and continue 0.5 mile east to another metal gate on the right; park in the small adjacent lot. The road beyond the gate is not as well maintained as the others described and is often muddy. Since fewer people visit this area, a walk along the road often produces Wild Turkeys. During spring and fall, the woodland you pass through as you start walking can abound with migrants. This is also one of the few places at McKee-Beshers where Louisiana Waterthrushes nest. After walking through the woods, you will arrive at a large field. At some distance on your left, near the edge of the woods, is a depression that is flooded regularly in spring and can be good for ducks and shorebirds. Recently, state authorities have built a small dike here which should make it a more reliable wetland. Beyond the first field are two smaller fields separated by strips of woodland. Walking through these three fields—usually planted in soybeans, corn, or sunflowers and millet—can be profitable. There are also small strips of other herbaceous plants that may attract sparrows, nesting Common Yellowthroats, and Indigo Buntings. Since the road ends at the third field, you must retrace your steps to your car.

A short drive up the hill brings you back to River Road. Turn right and drive about 0.4 mile to a grassy parking lot. During the nesting season, the overgrown area in front of the lot can yield White-eyed Vireo, Yellow-breasted Chat, Orchard Oriole, and possibly Blue Grosbeak. This is also the eastern edge of the main Prairie Warbler nesting area, which extends along River Road to Hughes Road. For adventurous souls, there is a large field surrounded mostly by forest to the south to explore. The path that begins after you go around the metal gate leads you into this field. You can either continue circling the field or turn left and walk until you reach the woods. This area is seldom birded, so there may be surprises.

For the final walk, drive west (left) on River Road, checking the overhead wires along the way. From July through September, large numbers of swallows, mainly Northern Rough-winged, gather there. Drive 0.3 mile past Hughes Road and turn left on Sycamore Landing Road. Another 0.2 mile brings you to a parking lot on the right. Park and start walking back toward River Road. Look for a metal gate on the right; walk past it to a shelter surrounded by large oak trees. At one time this was a reliable place to find wintering Red-headed

Woodpeckers, but in recent years they have been present only sporadically. The area can also be good for migrants. There are large fields on either side of the road as you approach River Road. In spring, the field on the left is often filled with water and is a good place to find American Bitterns and Common Snipe. In March, look here after dusk for displaying American Woodcock. Near the intersection with River Road is a grove of willow trees where a pair of Yellow Warblers and a pair of Willow Flycatchers often nest. Usually a pair of Blue Grosbeaks is also in this vicinity. In winter, Red-tailed Hawks often perch in the taller trees along the road, and both fields can be good for sparrows.

Return to the parking lot and walk about 0.5 mile south to the C&O Canal at Sycamore Landing. As you do so, you cross two small bridges where Eastern Phoebes often nest. The wooded, swampy area on the right side extends west to the Summit Hill Turf Farm. This is the original McKee-Beshers area, donated to the State of Maryland by local farmers. In early April, Yellow-crowned Night-Herons often feed near the second bridge. As you approach Sycamore Landing, the road is lined with bush honeysuckle and larger trees, which are often filled with birds, including nesting White-eyed Vireos and American Redstarts. Y

—*Paul Woodward*

Major Hunting Seasons:

The early dove season starts on September 1 and runs into late October; hunting is not allowed before noon, so mornings are available to birders. This is followed by the bow-and-arrow deer season on September 15. Since the vegetation is usually thick at this time, hunting is limited. Squirrel season starts the first week in October and ends in late January. Rabbits and quail are hunted in early November, but since neither species is common here, hunting opportunities are limited. Firearm deer season runs from the last Saturday in November to the second Saturday in December. The final season to be aware of is the spring turkey season—for bearded birds only—which runs from mid-April to mid-May. Hunting is allowed only from sunrise until noon, so birding is possible in the afternoon.

Further details about all hunting seasons can be found by viewing the Maryland Department of Natural Resources Web site (**www.dnr.state.md.us/wildlife**) or by calling the Maryland Wildlife and Heritage Division at **301–258–7308**.

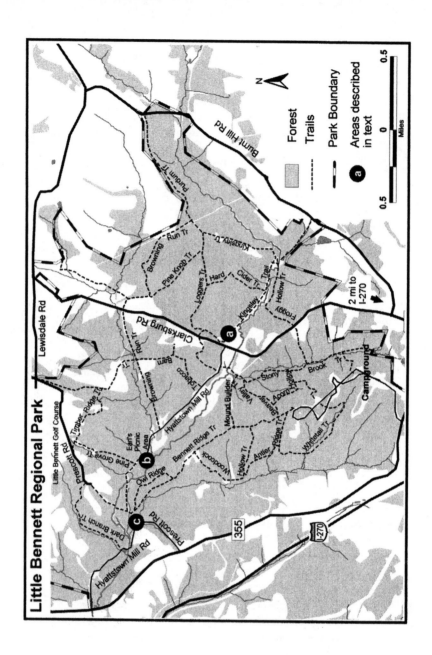

Little Bennett Regional Park

Forest
Trails
Park Boundary
Areas described in text

0.5   0   0.5
Miles

Little Bennett Regional Park, Clarksburg

Little Bennett

Best birds:
Woodpeckers, thrushes/ forest species, vireos/ warblers, sparrows

Habitat:
Mostly wooded, some fields along stream valleys

Conditions:
Portions hilly; equestrian trails muddy/rough; closed briefly during annual deer harvest (late fall); buggy in summer

Best seasons:
Spring and fall migrations

Amenities:
One portable toilet; gas stations near park

L ittle Bennett Regional Park's 3,700 acres offer numerous trails with good birding. Many of these trails are heavily wooded and hilly, so for diversity of habitat as well as ease of walking, birders have traditionally chosen to explore the stream valley section of the park, along Little Bennett Creek. There is no fee to use this area of the park, and it is open from dawn until sundown. To explore other trails you will need a trail map, obtainable at the campground entrance contact station north of Clarksburg Road on Route 355. The Park Manager's Office number is 301–972–9222.

Directions: From I-270, take exit 18, Clarksburg Road (Route 121), toward Clarksburg. Drive east for 2.6 miles, crossing Frederick Road (Route 355) as you go. The parking lot is at the bottom of a long hill, just after the bridge over Little Bennett Creek, on your right.

For Prescott Road, take exit 18, head east on Clarksburg Road (Route 121), and turn left (north) on Frederick Road (Route 355). Prescott Road is 2 miles ahead on your right.

Facilities: Sparse, except for a portable toilet at a Boy Scout campground about 1.5 miles from Kingsley Trail parking lot. There are also bathrooms at the campground off Route 355, about one mile north of the intersection with Route 121. Little Bennett is one of the most undeveloped parks in the area, and it is a good idea to take a water bottle if you are planning to spend several hours in the park.

Brief History: The Little Bennett Creek Valley has a long history. The northern part of the park, near Hyattstown, features a restored grist mill dating back to the 1790s. During the 1800s, there were also at various times a sawmill, a sumac mill, a bone-crushing mill to make fertilizer, and a whiskey distillery along Little Bennett Creek. A community of small farms arose in the stream valley, and the one-room Kingsley Schoolhouse was built in 1893. The schoolhouse was used until 1935, when the Great Depression forced most families to leave the Little Bennett region. In the 1960s, Montgomery County and the M-NCPPC began acquiring the land that would eventually form the park.

Area (a) Kingsley Trail: Park as directed above and scan the large shrubby field between the parking lot and Little Bennett Creek before starting down the trail. Check overhead for raptors; a Cooper's Hawk was seen one fall. At various times of the year, this field contains resident Song and Field sparrows, Common Yellow-throats, and Goldfinches, as well as migrant sparrows, including White-throated, Swamp, and occasionally Lincoln's. Other birds seen in this field include Yellow Warbler, Orchard Oriole, Indigo Bunting, and Willow Flycatcher. Just past the parking lot on the left side of Kingsley Trail is an open area where Prairie Warblers nest most years. A little farther along, on the right, is another shrubby field worth walking into. Until 1998, Blue-winged Warblers were reliable nesters here, but they have not been seen recently. However, Yellow-breasted Chat can usually be heard and, with patience, seen, as well as White-eyed Vireo, Yellow Warbler, and Blue-gray Gnatcatcher. In the fall, both Nashville and Palm warblers show up most years.

Back on the trail, check the small trees for foraging warblers in spring or fall. In 1998, migrating Blackburnian Warblers and a Golden-winged Warbler were seen in the walnut saplings along the trail. Yellow-rumped Warblers and an occasional "Baypoll" have also been seen here in late September.

Ignoring the din of catbirds, towhees, and cardinals, continue a few more yards; a footpath to the right leads down to the creek. The creek is worth looking at for its own sake, and you may see something interesting in the willow oaks and sycamores as well. In the early spring, the grass is low enough that you can negotiate a path along the creek for a few hundred yards before rejoining Kingsley Trail; after May, the grass is waist-high and wet, so it is best to return to the trail.

This part of the trail offers occasional good views into the understory both to the left and right. Anything is possible, from Hermit Thrush, Winter Wren, and both kinglets in the colder months to ubiquitous White-eyed and Red-eyed vireos, Eastern Wood-Pewee, and Acadian Flycatcher all summer long. Both Black-billed Cuckoo and Rose-breasted Grosbeak have been seen in migration. By mid-April, Northern Parulas are singing in the large sycamores by the creek. Resident Yellow-billed Cuckoos and Veeries are possible along this stretch as well, more often heard than seen. The steep slope on the left is favored by Ovenbirds, Wood Thrush, and other migrating thrushes. In the winter, Great Horned Owls can often be heard calling from the pines beyond the creek to your right.

About 0.5 mile from the parking lot, the trail dips and turns before rising again. Migrant warblers have been seen to the left near this dip, and Pileated Woodpeckers and Northern Flickers nest near here. The large dead tree trunks have numerous holes worth a look. Passing the Hard Cider Trail (equestrian) on the left, the trail straightens out for a few hundred yards, with large red oaks, tulip trees, and hickories towering above. Possible birds here include Yellow-throated Vireo, Carolina Wren, Wood Thrush, American Redstart, Eastern Towhee, an occasional Veery, and migrating Black-throated Blue, Canada, and Magnolia warblers. Eventually, the trail curves left near a rocky outcropping that supports beautiful wild columbine in April and May. At this point the creek and Kingsley Trail are only yards apart, and it's sometimes best to pause here hoping to see or hear nesting Louisiana Waterthrushes, Kentucky Warblers, and Belted Kingfishers. In two areas where the large trees are some distance back from the trail, it's worth checking them from this vantage point in the spring to avoid "warbler neck."

Beyond some mature walnut trees is a large field (often wet) favored by Indigo Buntings, Goldfinches, and various sparrows. Just past the field you will come to a T-junction. To the left is the Kingsley Trail and to the right the Froggy Hollow Schoolhouse. Turn right to spend a little time at this picturesque spot where a swinging bridge crosses the creek. Wood Ducks sometimes perch in a tree near the bridge, or they may flush from the creek. Eastern Phoebes usually nest under the schoolhouse eaves, while migrant warblers are attracted to the large trees in the grassy areas. Beyond the schoolhouse to the left, both Louisiana Waterthrush and Kentucky Warbler can usually be heard, if not always seen.

Return to the T-junction and head uphill on Kingsley Trail. This leads to a hilltop meadow where Prairie Warblers, Yellow-breasted Chats, Field Sparrows, Brown Thrashers, and Indigo Buntings often nest, and Nashville, Magnolia, and Palm warblers have been seen in migration. On the way up the hill, listen on your left for Ovenbirds and Worm-eating Warblers, both common in the wooded sections of the park. If they don't sound too far off, there are two trails that take you into the woods where you may see them. While climbing this hill, look for such migrant warblers as Black-throated Green, Black-throated Blue, Chestnut-sided, Blackburnian, and (rarely) Cape May. Notable nesters here include Yellow-billed Cuckoo, Yellow-throated Vireo, and Black-and-white Warbler.

It is possible to make a round trip of sorts by continuing on the trail past the primitive campground to the intersection with Logger's Trail. Take a left here and follow Logger's Trail through the woods for about a mile until it descends to the parking lot. All of the woodpeckers, including Hairy and Pileated, are possible here, as well as Brown Creeper and Winter Wren in the colder months. Most birders simply choose to return to the parking lot via Kingsley Trail, often seeing different birds than those seen earlier; it is certainly less strenuous this way. If you go as far as the campground (where the portable toilet is located), check the brushy areas for sparrows. Lincoln's Sparrow has been seen here in the past.

Area (b) Hyattstown Mill Road: Beginning across Clarksburg Road from the Kingsley Trail parking lot, this gravel road dead-ends after about a mile at Earl's Picnic Ground. There are several good birding spots along this end of the road. After passing a boggy field good for Red-winged Blackbirds, Willow and Great Crested flycatchers, and Eastern Kingbirds, turn left on a grassy path with a sign pointing toward the Beaver Valley Trail and the Nature Center. The small trees and shrubs at this turnoff are often good for migrant warblers.

Prairie Warblers nest beyond the evergreens to the right, but are easier to see farther down the road. Continue down the path (often wet with dew) until you approach a grove of young walnut trees on the right, with the Little Bennett Creek and a wooden bridge just ahead. Look here for Baltimore Orioles, Warbling and White-eyed vireos, Belted Kingfishers, Wood Ducks, and Great Crested Flycatchers. Ruby-throated Hummingbirds often perch on the top of the dead tree to the left of the path. Cross the wooden bridge, checking the bushes and trees ahead and to the left. When the morning sun hits these branches, Cedar Waxwings, Carolina Wrens, and migrant warblers are possible. Male Blackpoll and Canada warblers, inches apart, were once seen here in early May in a single binocular view!

A couple of hundred yards farther down Hyattstown Mill Road, there is a large field with a fenced enclosure and a bluebird box. For several years, this field has been a good spot to witness the courtship flight of the American Woodcock, usually beginning in early spring. While waiting for the woodcock to appear at dusk, one might also see resident Great Horned Owls in the tree line beyond the field or hear the call of a Whip-poor-will. Near Browning Run Trail (equestrian), open fields provide good vantage points to see Red-tailed Hawks—and at times, Red-shouldered Hawks—circling above. Cooper's Hawk has been sighted here in summer. One May, a birder sighted a Wild Turkey crossing the road.

Earl's Picnic Ground marks the end of Hyattstown Mill Road. In the fall, you may find Winter Wrens in the brush, both kinglets in the evergreens, and Fox Sparrows deeper in the woods. Nearby nesters have included Kentucky Warbler, Scarlet Tanager, and Yellow-billed Cuckoo.

The parking lot at Earl's Picnic Ground can serve as a starting point for an interesting two- or three-hour loop walk. The loop will take you through peaceful woods, varied fields, and clearings via Pine Grove Trail, Timber Ridge Trail, and Tobacco Barn Trail, ending at Hyattstown Mill Road, about three-quarters of a mile south of the picnic ground. Begin at Pine Grove Trail just beyond the road barricade and head uphill into a large grove of mature white pine trees, interspersed with young beech and tulip trees. The trail through the grove is mostly level, with good views uphill to the right and downhill to the left. Depending on the season, check for owls, kinglets, nuthatches, and Pine Warblers. Past the grove is an open area with good views into the trees in all directions. Then follow a grassy park road uphill for more good edge-birding possibilities. Check the shrubby areas for Prairie Warbler, Chat, and Field Sparrow. Turn right at the sign marked "Timber Ridge Trail to Tobacco Barn Trail."

As you re-enter the woods, scan the Virginia pines and, when you reach some open woods with good views on both sides, pause for a few minutes to look and listen. Both Pileated Woodpecker and Northern Flicker reside here year-round, with Wood Thrush and Scarlet Tanager in season. After passing through a grassy area, you will enter an impressive stand of tulip trees; descend toward a wooden bridge over a small creek where Louisiana Waterthrush, Ovenbird, Worm-eating Warbler, and Great Crested and Acadian fly-catchers are possible. At this point you will enter a large field of several acres, with a 19th-century log cabin on your left and a large, half-standing tobacco barn farther down a hill. The small and medium sized deciduous trees are worth examining for migrant warblers and resident Eastern Bluebirds and Indigo Buntings. Grasshopper

MOB '98

Louisiana Waterthrush

Sparrows have been sighted in this field. Continue on Tobacco Barn Trail, passing through lowland woods. Listen for Kentucky Warbler and Louisiana Waterthrush along Browning Run, a passable stream in dry weather but difficult to cross if it has rained recently.

Proceed straight ahead after crossing the Browning Run Trail and pass a hilly field on the right, where you may see a resident Red-tailed Hawk in the trees beyond the field. As you head back uphill through the woods, the trail comes to a T-intersection. Turn right here and begin descending toward Hyattstown Mill Road. Pine, Worm-eating, and Black-and-white warblers, Ovenbird, Scarlet Tanager, Veery, and Wood Thrush have been seen and heard along this stretch. Back on Hyattstown Mill Road, turn right and bird the easy three-quarter-mile walk back to your car. Blue-winged Warblers are still possible here. Look for resident Red-shouldered Hawks near the bridge over Browning Run, not far from Earl's Picnic Ground. A pair of Red-headed Woodpeckers was recently spotted in the field to the right of this bridge.

Area (c) Prescott Road: The north side of Little Bennett is much less used than the popular Kingsley Trail, but it is equally rewarding in number and variety of bird species. This area is best approached by turning right onto Prescott Road off Route 355. Park at the end of Prescott Road, where it makes a 90-degree left turn and continues as Hyattstown Mill Road.

The fields to your left are usually very birdy in all seasons. Fox Sparrow and Hermit Thrush have been seen here in late winter. Prairie and Blue-winged warblers, Yellow-breasted Chat, Indigo Buntings, and Field Sparrows frequent this area. Gray Catbird, Northern Cardinal, and White-throated Sparrow are common in the hedgerows. Red-shouldered Hawks nest along the creek.

Walk across the footbridge to your right, which spans Sopher's Branch. Kentucky and Parula warblers, as well as Redstart, Common Yellowthroat, and Louisiana Waterthrush, nest in this area. Eastern Phoebes usually nest under the bridge.

A bit farther down the path are the trailheads for the Bennett Ridge and Owl Ridge Trails. The Bennett Ridge Trail, which traverses a wide variety of habitats, also connects to a series of other park trails, including the Woodcock Hollow, Antler Ridge, Whitetail, Mound Builder, Beaver Valley, and Acorn Hollow trails. If you're especially ambitious and/or fit, you could hike over to the campground or all the way back to the trails on the other side of Clarksburg Road/ Route 121, discussed above. *A trail map is advisable if you're thinking of exploring this area of the park.* Any of the species previously mentioned can be found here. Blue-winged Warbler, Yellow-billed Cuckoo, Wood Thrush, Veery, and Worm-eating and Pine warblers are reliable nesters. A coyote was once spotted along the Bennett Ridge Trail.

The Owl Ridge Trail is a short loop notable for the native mountain laurel and pinxter azalea growing here. Worm-eating Warbler, Ovenbird, Wood Thrush, and Veery frequent this area in season. Other nesters include Great Crested Flycatcher, Eastern Wood-Pewee, and Scarlet Tanager. Migrant warbler species seen there include Blackburnian, Blackpoll, Chestnut-sided, Canada, Magnolia, Black-throated Blue, and Black-throated Green. Swainson's Thrushes pass through in good numbers during migration.

Returning to the Hyattstown Mill/Prescott Road intersection, continue down Hyattstown Mill Road. It's worthwhile to walk slowly down this road during spring and fall migrations; a birder recently tallied 15 species of warbler here on a spring morning.

As you cross a small bridge over Little Bennett Creek, look for the Dark Branch Trail on your right. Dark Branch Trail is a lovely, quiet woodland trail worth exploring for its own sake. You may find Worm-eating Warblers and Ovenbirds on the slopes along the trail, and Scarlet Tanagers and Indigo Buntings in the trees above. Acadian Flycatcher, Kentucky Warbler, and Louisiana Waterthrush nest here as well.

Finally, it should be mentioned that, when the doldrums of summer have dulled the birding, Little Bennett abounds in interesting butter-flies, including several beautiful hairstreaks and swallowtails and many challenging skippers. The tick-phobic however, may want to skip these months and return to the park in September. ⅄

—Mark England
(With thanks to Gemma Radko and Hugh Mahanes)

Song Sparrow

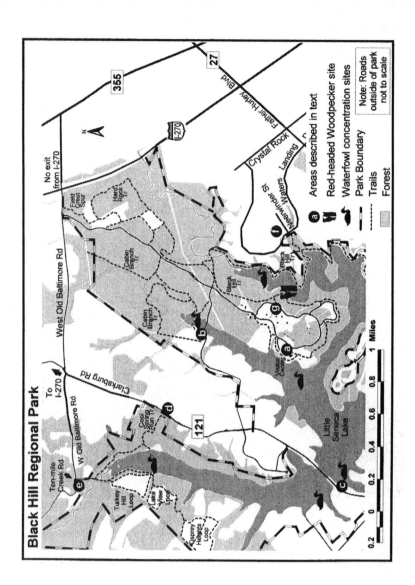

Black Hill Regional Park

355

27

Father Hurley Blvd

I-270

Crystal Rock

Landing

Neelsville Waters St

Areas described in text
Red-headed Woodpecker site
Waterfowl concentration sites
Park Boundary
Trails
Forest

Note: Roads
outside of park
not to scale

No exit
from I-270

N

Field Crest Spur

Hardt Road Tr.

Cabin Branch Tr.

Cabin Branch

West Old Baltimore Rd

Black Hill Tr.

Black Hill Tr.

g

b

Visitor Center

a

To
I-270

Clarksburg Rd

W. Old Baltimore Rd

Cool Spring Run Tr.

d

121

Ten-mile Creek Rd

e

Turkey Hill Loop

Lake View Loop

Osprey Heights Loop

Little Seneca Lake

c

0.2 0 0.2 0.4 0.6 0.8 1 Miles

Black Hill Regional Park, Boyds

C entered between Clarksburg, Germantown, and Boyds in western Montgomery County, Black Hill Regional Park is owned and managed by the M-NCPPC. Within its 1,843 acres birders will find a rich diversity of habitat: upland deciduous forest, stands of pine, old fields, wetlands (including streams, springs and marsh), mowed lawn areas, and hedgerows. The park surrounds Little Seneca Lake, created in 1984 as an emergency water supply for the greater Washington area. With its 15.7 miles of shoreline, the 505-acre lake has become one of the region's premier spots for observing wintering waterfowl.

Amenities: The park is open March 1–October 31 from 6 a.m. to official sunset and November 1–February 28 from 7 a.m. to official sunset (closed on Christmas and New Year's Day). All facilities are wheelchair accessible. In addition to the 10 miles of natural-surface trails, there are several miles of handicapped-accessible paved trails, a wheelchair-accessible fishing pier and a boat rental facility. Comfort stations are open only March 1–October 31; portable toilets are available year-round at the public boat ramp parking area. There is a pay telephone outside the Visitor Center. The park has no snack bar, but there are soda machines at some comfort stations. The closest store is Boyds Country Store.

Site at a Glance

Black Hill

Best birds:
Waterfowl, woodpeckers

Habitat:
Lake, woods, fields

Conditions:
Well-maintained trails, some paved; windy in winter

Best seasons:
Winter

Amenities:
Visitor center open weekends year-round; other restrooms open in season; picnic areas and boat rentals

Directions: From I-270, take exit 18, Clarksburg Road (Route 121), southwest towards Boyds. Drive 1.5 miles to West Old Baltimore Road (there will be a sign to the park), and take a sharp left. (The turn is on a curve; exercise caution.) Continue for 1.0 mile to the park entrance on your right. Follow this road, Lake Ridge Drive, 1.8 miles to the Visitor Center, on your right.

Black Hill Visitor Center: Hours may vary, depending on staff availability. It is generally open 11 a.m.–6 p.m. seven days a week from March 1– October 31, and 11 a.m.–5 p.m. on weekends only for the remainder of the year. Inside are restrooms, a water fountain, informational bulletin boards, displays, wildlife checklists, and trail maps. Be sure to allow time to visit the Claudia Wilds Library, with its extensive collection of bird and natural history books. If the center is closed, trail guides, bird checklists, and *Nutshell News* program guides are available in a literature rack located on the wall to the right of the front door. Staff naturalists conduct a variety of interpretive birding programs (including pontoon boat rides on the lake) year round; reservations and a nominal fee are required. Also, be sure to check the list of weekly bird sightings posted in the kiosk in the parking lot.

Birding Highlights:

- Ｙ Eastern Bluebirds: year-round; high productivity from extensive, monitored nest-box trails; all field areas.

- Ｙ Red-headed Woodpeckers: year-round; Cabin Branch area, Ten-mile Creek area, Black Hill Trail in Lake Churchill area, park area across road from Park Office.

- Ｙ Wading birds: Great Blue and Green herons, Great Egret, and others; lake shore in many locations.

- Ｙ Common Loons: northbound migration; deep coves on both sides of Clarksburg Road bridge, lake near Park Police boat house, lake near Visitor Center.

- Ｙ Waterfowl: ducks, geese, and swans in large numbers; 33 species recorded from 1990 to 2001; lake by bridge, lake by Visitor Center, Ten-mile Creek area.

The best areas for observing birds—the rear deck of the Visitor Center, the gravel parking lot across from the public boat ramp, the parking lot adjacent to Clarksburg Road bridge, the Ten-mile Creek area trails, and the Waters Landing area—are described in detail below. Letters refer to locations on the map.

Area (a) Visitor Center: One of the best locations for viewing gulls, wintering waterfowl, hawks during fall migration, and Bald Eagles December through February is the center's rear deck. You'll need a scope and an extra layer of clothing to block the wind that almost always blows off the lake. From this vantage point in winter you may see 20 or more waterfowl species. Regulars include Bufflehead, Ring-necked Duck, Canada Goose, Tundra Swan, Mallard, Pied-billed Grebe, and Ruddy Duck. Present in most years, but less abundant, are Northern Pintail, Canvasback, Gadwall, Red-breasted Merganser, Common Goldeneye, Long-tailed Duck, Red-throated Loon, and Horned Grebe. One winter a Trumpeter Swan visited the lake. Green-winged and Blue-winged teal are usually seen at the beginning and end of migration season. During the winter of 2000–01, a Harlequin Duck could be seen near the boat docks on an almost daily basis. The number of Common Loons stopping on the lake during spring migration increases each year. Most are in breeding plumage, and some can be heard yodeling on misty mornings.

As you leave the deck, check the seed and suet feeders located beside the building in the wildlife courtyard for Carolina Chickadee, Tufted Titmouse, White-breasted Nuthatch, Downy and Red-bellied woodpeckers, House Finch, and American Goldfinch. In previous winters, Pine Siskin, Common Redpoll, Red-breasted Nuthatch, and White-crowned Sparrow have occasionally visited these feeders. From late April to early October, check the hummingbird garden and feeders for Ruby-throated Hummingbirds.

Area (b) Public boat ramp gravel lot: After turning onto Lake Ridge Drive at the park entrance, continue past the small contact station shed and turn right on Black Hill Road. Cross over the lake and turn right into the large gravel parking lot. During warm weather, this overflow parking lot fills with boat and horse trailers, discouraging potential ground-nesters. But Killdeer are occasionally sighted in this area, so it's worth a look. The Cabin Branch Trail heads uphill from the left front edge of the parking lot, through fields and thickets where Eastern Bluebirds and Tree Swallows use the nesting boxes from April to August. Other likely birds are Indigo Bunting, Gray Catbird, Northern Mockingbird, Brown Thrasher, Northern Cardinal, Field and Song sparrows, and flocks of American Goldfinches and Cedar Waxwings. On one Christmas Count, a Yellow-breasted Chat made an appearance in a thicket of multiflora rose along this trail. In September, scan the skies above this high point for kettling Broad-winged Hawks. In November, watch for the occasional Golden Eagle flyover.

Another unnamed trail (made by fishermen) leads downhill from the right rear corner of the parking lot towards the rock jetty. Stop along the lake edge to scan the standing dead trees in the lake for Red-headed Woodpeckers. During nesting season, other cavity nesters that can be seen here include Pileated, Red-bellied, and Downy woodpeckers, Eastern Bluebird, Tree Swallow, European Starling, and Wood Duck. During the summer months, you may also see Great Blue and Green heron, Belted Kingfisher, Mallard, and Canada Goose from the jetty. For several years, the geese have nested on top of the active beaver lodge near the jetty. During migration, look for Solitary Sandpiper and Greater Yellowlegs. In winter, Ring-necked Ducks, Mallards, American Wigeons, Gadwalls, Pied-billed Grebes, and Hooded Mergansers favor this spot. On a past Christmas Count, birders standing on the jetty observed a Barred Owl and two Screech Owls. If you visit this location at dawn or dusk on a weekday, you may be lucky enough to see the resident beavers or river otters. Use caution if you venture off the path from spring through autumn, as northern banded water snakes are abundant and northern copperheads occasionally bask on the rocks of the jetty.

Area (c) Parking lot adjacent to Clarksburg Road bridge: Return to the park entrance and turn left on West Old Baltimore Road. Follow it to the stop sign and turn left on Clarksburg Road (Route 121). Again, use caution at this dangerous intersection. Cross the bridge that spans the lake and immediately turn left into the small gravel parking lot. Due to the shallow water and abundance of hydrilla (invasive, exotic, submerged aquatic vegetation) in the cove just below and to the right of the parking lot, wintering dabbling ducks prefer this site for feeding. They can be viewed easily with binoculars from mid-November to mid-March. Look for Mallard,

Canvasback, and Green-winged Teal, along with American Coot and Pied-billed Grebe. The occasional Redhead and Northern Shoveler will also show up here. You will need a spotting scope to view the large rafts of Ruddy Ducks, Buffleheads, and Ring-necked Ducks frequenting the deeper water just off the point. In the deep water near the dam (southeast direction across lake) scan for Common Goldeneye, Long-tailed Duck, Common and Red-breasted mergansers, and the occasional Red-throated Loon. At the same time, check dead trees along the shoreline for perching Bald Eagles. They may also be observed hunting ducks, preying mostly upon the American Coots and Ring-necked Ducks. After scanning the lake on this side of the bridge, take your scope and cross Clarksburg Road. A narrow fisherman's trail will lead you down to the shoreline, where you'll have good views of the north end of the lake. Tundra Swans tend to congregate in this part of the lake, as do Common Loons.

Because of limited parking and accessibility, the Ten-mile Creek section of the park is the least visited, although this may change once the Black Hill Master Plan is implemented. With its varied habitats, this is the best area in the park to see a diversity of bird life in any season. There are two access points:

Area (d) Cool Spring Run Trail: About halfway between West Old Baltimore Road and the Clarksburg Road bridge, there is a trailhead for Cool Spring Run on the west side of Clarksburg Road (refer to park map). Park in the pull-off on the east side of the road and cross the road to the trailhead. This hilly trail will take you through stands of eastern red cedar and mature pine forest. Screech Owls may be seen in the red cedars and Great Horned Owls nest in the pines. This is a good location to search for wintering owls, such as Saw-whet and Long-eared. In the portion of this trail that borders the lake, a Northern Shrike was seen on the 1999 Christmas Count.

Area (e) Ten-mile Creek Road: From Clarksburg Road, turn west on West Old Baltimore Road, then turn left onto Ten-mile Creek Road (gravel). Respect the "No Parking" sign, and take care not to block the private driveway or the locked park gate. Walk down the road to the creek. There may be a temporary bridge; flooding and high water from beaver activity sometimes make crossing difficult or impossible. (However, the flooding creates good habitat for ducks and herons.) The surrounding wetland area sustains several species of amphibians; you'll be serenaded by a frog and toad chorus on humid spring evenings. Growing in abundance here are cardinal flower and spotted jewelweed, whose flowers lure Ruby-throated Hummingbirds to their nectar in late summer. Red-headed Woodpeckers have sometimes been seen or heard in the wetland areas to the left of the stream.

Continue down the road located on the other side of the stream. On your left is a spring where birds gather to drink and bathe. In summer, be sure to look for "puddle clubs" of butterflies imbibing moisture and nutrients from the wet mud. In winter, look for Winter Wrens, Bluebirds, Purple Finches, Yellow-rumped Warblers, and Cedar Waxwings along this section of trail and in its seeps.

When you reach the intersection of Turkey Hill Loop Trail, bypass it (it is extremely steep) and continue straight ahead. The road climbs gradually and in winter, when the trees are bare, you will have fantastic unobstructed views of the lake. This is one of the best spots for scoping wintering waterfowl on the water. Walk silently so as not to flush the ducks from the shore below you. The road ends at the lake edge and there is a bench where you can relax and take in the beauty of the scene. From here you have easier access to the Turkey Hill Loop Trail, which consists of mostly rolling terrain with open fields and bountiful hedgerows. The expected field birds can be seen, along with the occasional Wild Turkey. Visitors have also reported seeing red fox, gray fox, and coyote along this trail. In summer, butterfly enthusiasts may see more than 30 species of butterflies nectaring on wildflowers in the fields and woodland edges. The hilltops offer great views and good spots to scan the sky for hawks during autumn migration. If you prefer to walk further, you may continue on this series of three loop trails. The walk between the Lake View Loop and the Osprey Heights Loop will take you through a lush ravine to the water's edge, where in spring you may enjoy the songs of warblers, thrushes, Scarlet Tanager, and other forest birds. Take some time to enjoy the spring woodland wildflowers and ferns. Osprey Heights Loop continues through open fields, hedgerows, and forest edge.

Area (f) Waters Landing area: Even though this area is part of Black Hill Regional Park, it is most easily accessed from outside the park. A paved path along the lake edge affords close looks at waterfowl; this is also a reliable location for Red-headed Woodpecker. Exiting the park on Lake Ridge Drive, turn right onto West Old Baltimore Road. Follow it to its end at Route 355 and turn right. After 0.8 mile turn right onto Father Hurley Boulevard. Continue 1.5 miles and turn right onto Waters Landing Drive. In 0.7 mile you will reach the intersection with Neerwinder Street. Park here and take the paved trail beginning on Waters Landing Drive directly across from Neerwinder. Shortly after the path enters the woods you will come to a junction. Keep right and continue another 100 yards to an area where the lake will be visible on your left. Bird the path for about a mile, searching in the coves for Redhead, Bufflehead, Hooded Merganser, and Ring-necked and Wood ducks. Look in the clusters of dead trees for Red-headed Woodpecker. Retrace the trail back to your car.

Area (g) Best bet for Red-headed Woodpeckers: Several locations for Red-headed Woodpecker are mentioned above, but if you have limited time this might be your quickest and best chance to find this specialty species. Park in lot 9, marked (g) on the map. Enter the woods across the road from the lot; take a well-worn trail to access the Black Hill Trail and turn right. Proceed several hundred yards to the bottom of the hill where the lake comes into view. Leave the trail and search along the shore, checking clusters of dead trees standing in the water. You will often hear their harsh "queark" calls before seeing them. Retrace your steps to return to the lot. ⅄

—Denise Gibbs

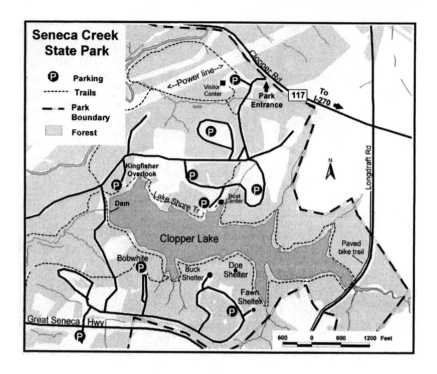

Seneca Creek State Park, Gaithersburg

A large stream valley park west of Gaithersburg, Seneca Creek State Park stretches for 12 miles along Great Seneca Creek and features the 90-acre Clopper Lake. On warmer weekends, the lake area draws picnickers, mountain bikers, and canoeists; far fewer people visit during the week. Birding a relatively small portion of the park for almost three years, I have identified more than 150 species, including Hooded Warbler, Wild Turkey, and Gray-cheeked Thrush.

There is an entrance fee of $1 per person on weekends and holidays, May to September. The park, with its several miles of marked trails, is open from 8 a.m. to sunset. The Visitor Center (301–924–2127), open from 9 a.m. to 4 p.m. seven days a week, has trail maps and rest rooms. Parking areas are scattered throughout the park.

Directions: From I-270 northbound, take exit 10, Clopper Road (Route 117). Follow Clopper west 2.2 miles to the park entrance on your left.

From I-270 southbound, take exit 11, Quince Orchard Road (Route 124). From the exit ramp, turn right onto Quince Orchard and drive south 0.4 mile to the second traffic light, Clopper Road (Route 117). Turn right (west) onto Clopper and proceed 1.5 miles to the park entrance on the left.

The Area: Clopper Lake is the winter home or resting grounds for many species of waterfowl, and the lake's relatively small size provides satisfactory to excellent views

Site at a Glance

Seneca Creek State Park

Best birds:
Waterfowl, woodpeckers, thrushes/forest species

Habitat:
Lake, deciduous woods, mowed fields

Conditions:
Moderate to strenuous hiking, hilly, muddy after rain; closed briefly during annual deer harvest

Best seasons:
Winter for waterfowl

Amenities:
Scattered restrooms not always open; seasonally open boat center has restrooms, snack machines. No trash containers in park

of the birds, even without a spotting scope. During the winter, one can expect to see about 20 species of waterfowl, including Tundra Swan, all the dabblers except Northern Shoveler, large rafts of Ring-necked Ducks with a few Redheads and Lesser Scaup interspersed, Ruddy Duck, Bufflehead, and all three mergansers. Long-tailed Duck and Common Loon have also been seen here. Pied-billed and Horned grebes are regular visitors, as are Double-crested Cormorants and American Coots.

The shores of the lake host Great Blue Herons year round, with Green Herons joining them in summer. Both Black- and Yellow-crowned night-herons are seen on occasion. Belted Kingfishers frequently rattle past. During migration, Spotted and Solitary sandpipers and Common Snipe pick their way along the shoreline. One can spot Osprey, both vultures, and resident Red-shouldered and Red-tailed hawks overhead. In September, kettles of Broad-winged Hawks, sometimes numbering in the hundreds, are common. On fall mornings, it is not unusual to find a Broad-wing perched in a tree, resting before its trip southward. Both Barred and Great Horned owls may nest near the lake and, like Sharp-shinned and Cooper's hawks, make regular appearances. With luck, you might spot a Merlin atop a bare branch overlooking the water.

In winter, a walk through the wooded areas around the lake can often yield six species of woodpecker. The careful listener and observer can find Brown Creeper, Hermit Thrush, and both species of kinglet. Winter Wrens frequent the edge of the lake and its adjacent streams, as do Rusty Blackbirds. When Red-breasted Nuthatches venture this far south in winter, you are almost sure to hear their high-pitched "beeping" in conifers throughout the park.

Spring brings at least 25 species of nesting or migrating warblers, including Blue-winged, Wilson's, Bay-breasted, and Canada. At this time of year, all the expected thrushes and vireos pass through the park, as do Rose-breasted Grosbeaks, Scarlet Tanagers, Yellow-billed Cuckoos, and Ruby-throated Hummingbirds. Fall migrants include Fox Sparrow.

In summer, nesting sparrows and woodpeckers share the woodlands with flycatchers, thrushes, vireos, Blue-gray Gnatcatchers, and Cedar Waxwings. Common Yellowthroats and Prairie Warblers are conspicuous breeders in the park In the hotter months, the edges of the woods and fields are filled with Eastern Kingbirds, thrashers, Eastern Bluebirds, wrens, and orioles, while insect-eating birds patrol the lake.

The Lake Shore Trail: The 3.7-mile Lake Shore Trail, which encircles Clopper Lake, begins in front of the Kingfisher Overlook parking lot. To reach it, drive 0.2 mile past the entrance booth, bear right, and go 0.5 mile past the Cardinal and Chickadee picnic areas to the King-fisher Overlook sign. Turn left into the parking area, which can be great for warblers and Scarlet Tanagers in spring.

The full route suggested below may take four hours or more, but you can break up the long hike by driving from one parking lot to another and making short jaunts to the lake and back. Another alternative is to hike just the lower half of the trail, doubling back more directly and quickly.

A trail to your right (as you face the water) heads to the dam at the west end and to the most scenic view of Clopper Lake. Although the light is not always good for birding and you will need a scope in order to see most of the waterfowl, it is worth a stop just for the beautiful vista. Return to the lot and walk left, following the blue-blazed trees marking the Lake Shore Trail. As you go down the hill, look and listen for buntings, sparrows, American Redstart, and Common Yellowthroat. (It was here in spring 2000 that I was fortunate enough to see 17 warbler species in one hour!) Just across a short wooden bridge, a path to the right leads to the water. There are seldom many ducks in this little cove but check the shoreline for sandpipers.

Back on the main trail, you soon come to a field; walk its perimeter, beginning on your left. Cross the playground and head back down toward the lake. This area is good for sparrows, orioles, mimic thrushes, and nesting Prairie Warblers. This end of the lake often holds American Coots, dabblers, and even a Redhead or two.

The trail next takes you through a small section of woods where common backyard birds reside and where Pine Siskins and Purple Finches have been found. Ahead, the trail splits into three routes, all of which lead to the Boat Center. (There's a drink machine outside the Boat Center, and if the center is open you can buy snacks at a vending machine.)

Regain the trail at the corner of the parking lot beyond the Boat Center, on your right. As you enter the woods bear left, following the blue blazes and listening for nuthatches, flycatchers, and vireos. A short hike will bring you to the tip of one of the lake's fingers. Following the trail farther will lead you to a bridge. At this point you can either make a left and detour uphill to a peony field, or continue across the bridge. If you want to head back to your car, go uphill through the peony field, make a left at the road and follow it back to the Kingfisher Overlook. To continue, cross the bridge and follow the trail to your left, which takes you over a hill. At the bottom, you will have a good view of the east end of the lake, where ducks tend to congregate.

The trail leads through a stand of pines to the northeast corner of the lake, then continues alongside a stream. Take the bridge across the stream, turn left, and leave the path to walk along the stream, looking for Winter Wrens. Back on the trail, cross the wide gravel path and head uphill to your right. Along the left side of the trail is another large group of pine trees—the best place in the park to find Barred Owl. You will almost always see deer here, often in large numbers. The trail then continues around the stream and up a small hill. From the peak of the hill, go down to the edge of the lake for another good view of any ducks in the water.

Return to the trail and follow it up a hill to the paved bicycle path that runs along the side of Longdraft Road. Turn right onto the bike path and walk about 100 yards to the last pair of "No Parking" signs. Cross the street (look both ways) and walk between the split in the guard rail. Descend the steep hill, looking for Eastern Phoebe and Swamp Sparrow. As you cross the cement walkway, scan the water for herons, Rusty Blackbirds, waterthrushes, and Wood Ducks. The woods to the right are worth exploring for migrating thrushes and possibly a Great Horned Owl. Continue straight ahead on the path, until you begin to see homes—the edge of park property.

To get back to the Lake Shore Trail, turn around, go back up the steep hill and recross the street. The split in the guard rail to your left is the trailhead. You will now have covered the southern half of

Canada Goose

the Lake Shore Trail. You can either return the way you came (or via the peony field), leaving the trail occasionally to examine more carefully habitats previously uncombed, or continue around the lake.

The south side of the lake is not as active as the north, but if you have the time and energy it may bring a few nice sightings. From the south shore you can get good looks at waterfowl on the lake near Longdraft Road in the afternoon and evening. (You can also get there by parking near the Fawn picnic shelter and walking a short distance to the lake.) The coves on this side of the lake sometimes provide privacy for reclusive Wood Ducks. A good long hike will bring you to the dam. Enjoy the view, then cross the dam. You will notice steps leading up to the Kingfisher Overlook parking lot.

Other Trails: Five main trails loop through areas in the vicinity of the lake and the Visitor Center, most of which can be correctly labeled as "underbirded" and worthy of exploration. One of them, Long Draught Trail, leads into the new Seneca Greenway Trail, which follows Seneca Creek all the way to the Potomac River at Riley's Lock. Two trails (Great Seneca Trail and Old Pond Trail) start from the Visitor Center parking lot. To access the others, follow the entrance road past the entrance booth (noting one of the park's many bluebird boxes to the left of the booth), bear right at the stop sign, and continue to the Kingfisher Overlook parking lot. Ƴ

—Andy Rabin

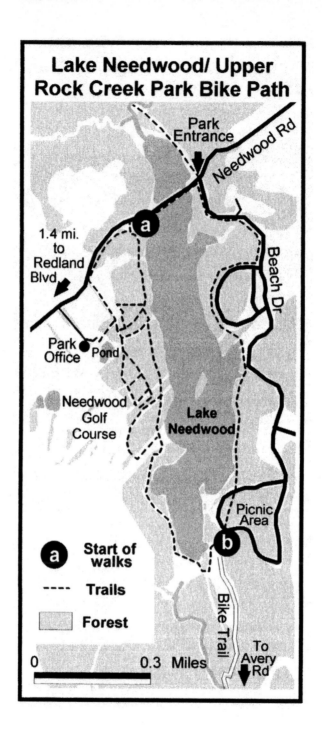

Lake Needwood/ Upper Rock Creek Park Bike Path

Park Entrance
Needwood Rd
1.4 mi. to Redland Blvd
Beach Dr
Park Office
Pond
Needwood Golf Course
Lake Needwood
Picnic Area
a Start of walks
---- Trails
Forest
0   0.3 Miles

Bike Trail
To Avery Rd

Site at a Glance

Lake Needwood/ Upper Rock Creek

Best birds:
Woodpeckers, thrushes/forest species, vireos/warblers

Habitat:
Field, lake, stream valley, deciduous woods

Conditions:
Hilly near the lake, relatively flat along Rock Creek bike path

Best seasons:
Spring, early summer

Amenities:
Restrooms in picnic areas

Although the Lake Needwood area of Rock Creek Regional Park focuses heavily on recreation, it also offers a wide range of birding habitats. On a busy weekend day, birders will encounter archers, bikers, rollerbladers, dog walkers, runners, soccer players, fishers, picnickers, golfers, and perhaps a fellow birder. Nevertheless, some spots are relatively untraveled and peaceful, and birders can spend two to six hours (even longer for the very thorough) in interesting exploration.

The habitats include mature deciduous woods along Rock Creek, brambles and overgrown meadows, open lake and lakeside, grass fields with occasional shrubs, some wetlands and vernal pools, and golf course edge.

Directions: From I-270, take exit 8, Shady Grove Road/Redland Boulevard. Bear right onto Redland and follow Redland as it crosses Frederick Road (Route 355). Continue east 0.9 mile to the traffic light at Needwood Road and turn right. From this intersection it is 1.4 miles to the lake and to some wide parking areas along the road. Park here if you are doing the first walk below. For the alternative starting point, continue 0.2 mile to the park entrance on your right, and follow the park road 1.2 miles (passing picnic areas 1 and 2) to the parking lot at the beginning of Rock Creek Hike/Bike path (this is very near the south end of the lake).

Amenities: This park has extensive picnic areas with restroom facilities, although none is near the best birding sites. In addition, the south end of the lake has a small Visitor Center that rents paddle boats and sells snacks in summer. The usual fast food chains are a short drive away along Frederick Road or Shady Grove Road, or at the corner of Redland Road and Muncaster Mill Road.

Walk (a): The first walk begins where Needwood Road meets the lake. In fall and winter the lake may have a variety of waterfowl (though they are neither as numerous nor as varied as at Black Hill). Good finds include scaup, Hooded Mergansers, Ring-necked Ducks, and Wood Ducks. Canada Geese are present in large numbers all year. In summer (particularly late summer) look for egrets and turtles. If water levels are low in the small area of lake north of the road, there may be shorebirds such as yellowlegs and peeps. Cliff Swallows nest under the small bridge just before the park entrance, and Tree Swallows, Rough-winged Swallows, and Chimney Swifts are present from spring through summer.

An obvious trail begins at the west edge of the lake, just a few yards from the road. After it enters the woods, bear left and walk through the woods above the lake. In some places you can get down to the lakeside for a better look at waterbirds. Soon you will come to trails that lead uphill through scrubby woods and into a very overgrown meadow between the lake and the Needwood Golf Course. This area hosts several pairs of nesting Prairie Warblers and one or more pairs of nesting Yellow-breasted Chats. In spring the fields and wood edges can be excellent for migrants. The golf course edges seem particularly good for migrating warblers, especially Tennessee, and for Baltimore Orioles. This is also a good spot for Eastern Bluebird, American Goldfinch, and Indigo Bunting and, in winter, lots of White-throated Sparrows. After exploring these fields and woods, work back to the trail along the lakeside; the woods here are the best spot for Scarlet Tanager.

MOB   *American Goldfinch*

Eventually the trail comes out at the south end of the lake and crosses the large earthen dam that forms the lake. You are now at the start
of the Rock Creek Hike/Bike Path described in **Walk (b)** below. You
could return the way you came, but if you have another two hours
the longer walk via the park road takes you through mature woods
and some very nice grass fields with scattered shrubs. These fields
are always worth searching for sparrows (Field and Song are common), Orchard Oriole, and raptors such as Red-tailed Hawk.
Occasionally a Black Vulture makes an appearance among the much
more common Turkey Vultures. The mature woods along the road
are another good spot for migrating warblers. At Needwood Road,
you can return to your car or you can cross the road and walk back
along the gravel road at the shallow north end of the lake to check
again for herons, shorebirds, swallows, and Wood Ducks.

If you have another two hours or so, there are a number of informal trails that wind through the woods. A reasonably easy one to follow runs right along Rock Creek, where you might find Prothonotary Warbler as well as turtles, snakes, and salamanders. This is a somewhat isolated wooded stretch that might best be explored with a friend.

Walk (b): This two-mile walk to Old Baltimore Road begins in the parking lot at the start of the Rock Creek Hike/Bike path. The paved path provides easy walking as it runs through mature woods along the banks of Rock Creek. On a quiet weekday at any season except late summer it is beautiful and birdy. On busy weekends you will have to be very careful to dodge bikers, runners, dogs off the leash, rocketing bladers, and the ubiquitous and sometimes speeding deer. If all that commotion doesn't bother you, this walk can be fascinating. It is a great area for birding by ear and for general woods appreciation.

In spring and summer the woods are full of woodland birds, including Yellow-billed Cuckoo, Red-eyed Vireo, Acadian Flycatcher, Blue-gray Gnatcatcher, Northern Parula, American Redstart, and Scarlet Tanager. Louisiana Waterthrushes nest along the creek and generally can be heard in the stretch between the parking lot and Southlawn Lane (first of two road crossings on this walk). But especially pleasing are the many nesting Wood Thrushes, whose songs fill the woods until late summer, and the choruses of frogs heard on warm days from February until April. Listen any time of year in these wet woods for Barred Owls and, in season, the occasional Veery. The many vernal pools along the path present good opportunities for "herping;" if you are very lucky, you may see a copperhead slithering across the path. As along the lake, this walk is excellent in winter for searching out the small mixed feeding flocks of chickadees, nuthatches, kinglets, woodpeckers, and titmice. Also look for Winter Wren.

A few hundred yards after crossing Avery Road, the path bends sharply right. At this corner, a dirt path on the left goes uphill to Lake Bernard Frank, where additional areas could be explored. The main path eventually leads all the way to Mount Vernon, but turning around at Old Baltimore Road seems reasonable and makes for a round-trip walk of just over four miles. Υ

—*John Bjerke*

Veery

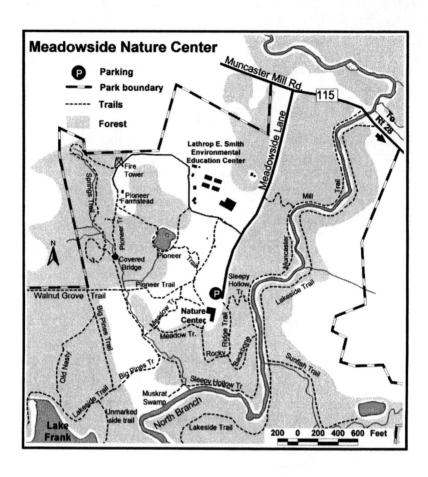

Meadowside Nature Center

P Parking
━━━ Park boundary
----- Trails
▨ Forest

Muncaster Mill Rd

115

To Rt 28

Lathrop E. Smith Environmental Education Center

Fire Tower

Pioneer Farmstead

Springs Trail

Pioneer Tr

Meadowside Lane

Mill

Trail

Muncaster

N

Covered Bridge

Pioneer

Pioneer Trail

Sleepy Hollow Tr.

Lakeside Trail

Walnut Grove Trail

Meadow Tr.

Nature Center

Meadow Tr.

Ridge Trail

Backbone

Big Pines Trail

Old Nasty

Lakeside Trail

Big Pines Tr

Rocky

Sunfish Trail

Sleepy Hollow Tr

Muskrat Swamp

Unmarked side trail

North Branch

Lakeside Trail

Lake Frank

200 0 200 400 600 Feet

Meadowside Nature Center, Rockville

P art of Rock Creek Regional Park, Meadowside Nature Center offers 2,700 acres of varied habitat. The Nature Center building (301–924–4141) is open 9 a.m.–5 p.m., Tuesday–Saturday. Inside, you will find trail maps, nature exhibits, bird and amphibian lists, and restrooms. Should you hear a sudden chorus of Barred and Great Horned owls, temper your excitement, as there are a number of injured raptors caged behind the center. The trails are open daily from sunrise to sunset. There is a portable toilet in the parking lot.

Directions: From I-270, take exit 6A, West Montgomery Avenue (Route 28), east toward Rockville. Follow Route 28 for 1.5 miles to the first traffic light past Rockville Pike (Route 355). At the light, turn left to stay on Route 28 (here called First Street, it will become Norbeck Road). In another 4.0 miles, turn left onto Muncaster Mill Road (Route 115). Continue 1.4 miles, turn left at Meadowside Lane, and drive 0.4 mile to the Nature Center parking lot.

From I-495, take exit 31A, Georgia Avenue (Route 97), and drive north. At 2.5 miles, you will cross University Boulevard. In another 5.4 miles, turn left onto Norbeck Road (Route 28). Take the first right onto Muncaster Mill Road (Route 115) and go 1.4 miles to the Meadowside Lane entrance described above.

Suggested Route: After you have checked the open expanse above the parking lot for soaring raptors, examine the surrounding

Site at a Glance

Meadowside

Best birds:
Waterfowl, woodpeckers, thrushes/forest species, vireos/warblers

Habitat:
Woods, meadows, lake

Conditions:
Moderately hilly

Best seasons:
Spring and fall migration

Amenities:
Restrooms in Visitor Center (closed Mondays), portable toilet outside

trees for flycatchers, vireos, and warblers in migration. The hill to the right as you face the Nature Center (northwest of the parking lot) can act as a migrant trap. The sun warms this ridge early, and birds may be active here before they disperse throughout the park. The following route will take you through some of the birdiest areas while keeping the sun at your back and could take a full morning.

The Pioneer and Meadow Trails are reached by climbing the gentle hill to the right of the Nature Center, passing a grove of paulownia trees on the right. Take the right branch to reach the Pioneer Trail. As the trail descends, look in the grasses and occasional conifers for sparrows, Indigo Buntings, and orioles in season. Walk down toward the small Pioneer Pond, noting in the background the large observation tower (locked) with its roosting Black and Turkey vultures.

Check the bushes and small trees near the Purple Martin house for White-eyed Vireo, Eastern Bluebird, Cedar Waxwing, Eastern Towhee, orioles, and American Goldfinch. The pond will probably hold Canada Geese and Mallards, but Great Blue and Green herons and Belted Kingfisher are also possible. Look here for Eastern Wood-Pewee and Eastern Kingbird. In migration, you could find Willow Flycatcher on the island in the center of the pond.

Go left around the pond, checking the trees and shrubs for bird activity. Take the small boardwalk that runs between the pond and a marsh (a split-rail fence keeps you out of the marsh itself). The marshy area can be good for vireos, warblers, and sparrows. At the end of the boardwalk, turn left past the brown sign marked "Sensitive Marsh Area—Please Keep Out." Continue up a small hill to a spot where the trail splits; either path leads to the Pioneer Farmstead.

The open area around the farmstead can be good for woodpeckers, flycatchers (Eastern Wood-Pewee, Acadian, Least, and Great Crested), wrens, warblers, and tanagers. Allow some time to bird this area; then take the gravel trail beyond the log cabin (heading right) to the observation tower for close-up views of the roosting vultures. Return the way you came, past the cabin, and continue on the gravel trail that leaves the farmstead area. The first path (unmarked) on the right leads to an overlook with a fine forest

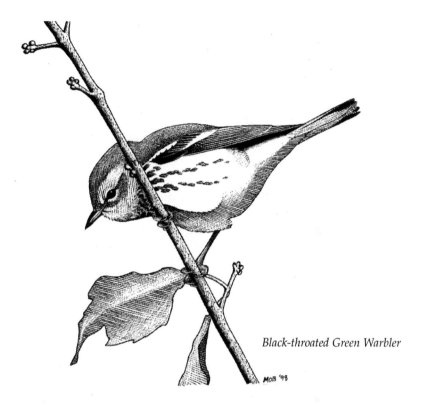

Black-throated Green Warbler

MOB '98

valley vista. Look here for vireos, thrushes, warblers (Blackburnian, Worm-eating, Ovenbird, and Kentucky are possible), and tanagers.

The trail then descends to a covered bridge; Eastern Phoebes usually nest under the roof. Just beyond the bridge, look for vireos, Blue-gray Gnatcatcher, warblers, and the occasional Barred Owl.

Bear left into an open meadow and proceed (right) up a gentle hill to Walnut Grove Trail. This area can be good for migrant warblers, including Black-and-white, Tennessee, Magnolia, Black-throated Blue, Black-throated Green, Cerulean, Chestnut-sided, Bay-breasted, and Palm. Northern Parula and Prairie Warbler, as well as American Redstart, nest in the area. In season, check for Yellow-billed Cuckoo, Ruby-throated Hummingbird, both kinglet species, Indigo Bunting, and Purple Finch.

Continue up Walnut Grove Trail to the T-intersection with Big Pines Trail at the top of the hill and turn left. In fall, check the fruit-bearing bushes for Gray Catbird, Northern Mockingbird, Brown Thrasher, and Cedar Waxwing. Prairie Warbler, Common Yellowthroat, and Yellow-breasted Chat are possible. Bear left onto Big Pines Trail, continuing through a mixed evergreen and deciduous woods to the intersection with Lakeside Trail (unmarked) where Cerulean, Hooded, and Kentucky warblers have been seen.

Bear right onto Lakeside Trail (marked by a blue-blazed tree on the right) and, a short distance beyond the intersection, follow the small path on the left through the woods that leads to the 54-acre Lake Frank. Scan the lake for Double-crested Cormorants, herons, egrets, and waterfowl. Look overhead for seasonal raptors—Osprey, Sharp-shinned, Cooper's, Red-shouldered, Broad-winged, or Red-tailed hawks are possible. Solitary and Spotted sandpipers, as well as Killdeer, might be seen on the shore. In winter, you may spot a Hooded or Red-breasted merganser on the lake.

Return to Lakeside Trail, turn right, and then right again onto Big Pines Trail in the direction of the Nature Center. Immediately after entering Big Pines Trail take a short detour on the overgrown, dead-end path to the left. Check this area during migration (Golden-winged Warbler is possible) and then return to the trail.

At the end of Big Pines Trail, there are two ways to get onto Sleepy Hollow trail, the final leg of the route. A left turn takes you through meadows to a grove of conifers on the left that may hold a roosting Barred Owl and (during migration) Red-breasted Nuthatch. A right turn will take you back to the Nature Center through deciduous woods.

When you come to a small wooden bridge, take the unmarked trail to the right to the muskrat swamp, a good area during migration for Hairy Woodpecker, Blue-headed Vireo, Blue-gray Gnatcatcher, and Northern Parula. Return to the wooden bridge, cross it, and continue along Sleepy Hollow Trail, keeping the creek on your right. This attractive section of the park is good for migrating cuckoos, vireos, warblers, Rose-breasted Grosbeak, Belted Kingfisher, and woodpeckers. Where the trail makes a sharp left, passing Rock Creek on the right, listen for Worm-eating and Hooded warblers and look for both Northern and Louisiana waterthrushes in migration. The area where the Backbone Trail leads off to the left (and there is a small section of split-rail fence on the right) is good for spring wildflowers and fall fungi.

From here, you can take the trail on the left that leads up the hill and straight back to the Nature Center, or you can descend the wooden steps, turn left, and bird the Muncaster Mill Trail, excellent in early spring for migrants and in all seasons for woodpeckers. This trail ends at Muncaster Mill Road, so you must return the way you came, back up the steps and along the trail to the Nature Center. Y

—*Ted Vawter*

Swamp Sparrow

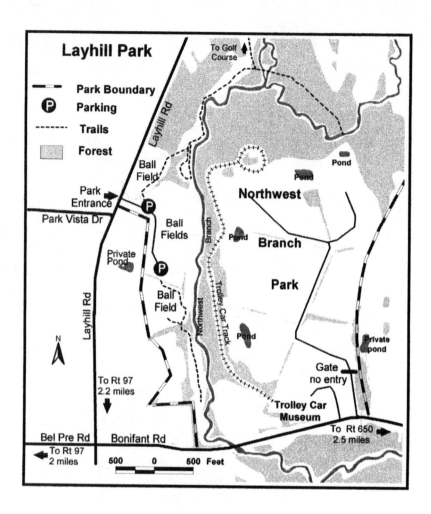

Layhill Park

— · — Park Boundary

🅿 Parking

----- Trails

▨ Forest

Layhill Rd

To Golf Course

Ball Field

Park Entrance

Park Vista Dr

Ball Fields

Private Pond

Ball Field

Layhill Rd

N

To Rt 97 2.2 miles

Bel Pre Rd   Bonifant Rd

To Rt 97 2 miles

Northwest Branch

Pond

Pond

Northwest Branch Park

Pond

Trolley Car Track

Pond

Private pond

Gate no entry

Trolley Car Museum

To Rt 650 2.5 miles

500   0   500 Feet

Layhill Park, Layhill

L ayhill Park is a multi-use area set into
Northwest Branch Park. Although fre-
quented by few birders over the years, the
area now offers some of the more rustic woodland and hedge habitats remaining in heavily
suburbanized east/central Montgomery
County. As of this writing, the areas adjacent
to the park retain a rural feel. The park is
flanked to the west by a small farm (and
Layhill Road), to the north by a public golf
course, to the east and south by the National
Capital Trolley Museum, new houses, and a
larger farm.

Directions: From I-495, take exit 31A,
Georgia Avenue (Route 97), and drive north.

At 3.4 miles, turn right onto Layhill Road
(Route 182). Take Layhill 3.9 miles to the
park entrance, marked by a brown sign, on
the right.

From I-270, take exit 4A, Montrose Road,
and drive east. At 2.1 miles you will cross
Rockville Pike (Route 355), where Montrose
Road becomes Randolph Road. At 1.9 miles
you will cross Veirs Mill Road; another 1.8
miles will bring you to Georgia Avenue
(Route 97). Turn left (north) on Georgia and
drive 0.2 mile to Layhill Road. Turn right on
Layhill and drive 3.9 miles to the park
entrance.

The Area: Much of the park visible from the
parking lots consists of playing fields and
rough, unmown edge abutting the woods of
Northwest Branch. The mown areas around
the playing fields and parking lots are dotted

Layhill Park

Best birds:
Woodpeckers,
thrushes/forest species,
vireos/warblers, sparrows

Habitat:
Deciduous woods, shrub-
by overgrown fields

Conditions:
Difficult—muddy, rough,
brambles, ticks; high
boots advised for stream
crossings

Best seasons:
Fall, winter, spring

Amenities:
Portable toilets

with scattered red cedar, white pine, and other trees that attract migrants and Eastern Bluebirds, which nest in the park's boxes. Two main paths, one accessible from the north parking lot (nearest Layhill Road) and one just south of the south parking lot, provide access to the wooded interior along Northwest Branch.

Layhill Park is at its best during spring and fall migrations, when all the northeastern vireos and most of the eastern warblers pass through in moderate numbers, thrushes frequent the swampy woods along the streams, and Rose-breasted Grosbeaks and surprise rarities may be seen. While numbers cannot compare to such hotspots as the DC section of Rock Creek Park, the diligent birder is bound to come away with an impressive list of songbird migrants. A few Mourning Warblers and Lincoln's Sparrows turn up every year or so. A Sedge Wren even popped up in a wet field, and Savannah and Vesper sparrows sometimes make an appearance. In May, Bobolinks may frequent the trees and field around the small house, farm, and waste yard between the parking lots and Layhill Road.

While birding the open areas, always keep an eye to the sky. Many birds fly over, following the north-to-south green ribbon of Northwest Branch Park. During hawk migration, small kettles of Broad-winged Hawks and small numbers of Sharp-shinned and Cooper's hawks, Osprey, and Northern Harrier often pass by. Though rarely having reason to land, Ring-billed Gulls, Canada Geese, Turkey and Black vultures, and Great Blue Herons float and flap over. Unusual fly-bys have included Common Mergansers and Double-crested Cormorants.

A variety of other wildlife takes refuge in the park. Beaver sign is abundant, and occasionally one of these ponderous rodents makes an appearance. White-tailed deer, chipmunk, gray squirrel, cottontail rabbit, groundhog, and red fox live here too. In late summer, the park's clearings, rich in thistle and other wildflowers, harbor a bounty of butterflies. This part of Northwest Branch contains one of the few remaining brown trout streams in the area. (Brown trout, an introduced species, require clean water for spawning.)

Ball Fields: For the early birder, the parking lot and ball field edges offer good places to start. Before the sports teams arrive, the lot area is alive with birds. Field, Song, and Chipping sparrows favor the gravelly shoulder around the baseball field. From May to early October, orioles, vireos, gnatcatchers, bluebirds, and kingbirds sing or cavort in the many deciduous trees that edge the surrounding woods, while Eastern Towhee, Gray Catbird, Indigo Bunting, and Common Yellowthroat are common in the tall grass and multiflora rose growing in the rough buffer strips between fields and woods. Red-winged Blackbirds and, in season, Swamp Sparrows frequent the patch of cattails near the south parking lot.

The Red-shouldered Hawk is Layhill Park's most frequently observed resident raptor. A Barred Owl or two is usually around, roosting in some of the larger trees in the woods. Red-tailed Hawk, American Kestrel, Eastern Screech Owl, and Great Horned Owl put in regular appearances (the owls at night, of course). A Merlin sometimes makes a fall or winter appearance.

Along the stream edge, Wood Ducks, Green Herons, and one or two Belted Kingfishers are often present. Keep an eye out for migrating Solitary and Spotted sandpipers as well. In late fall and winter, Winter Wrens often hang around the fallen logs and tangles along the eroded stream bank. Other notable cold-weather visitors include Rusty Blackbirds in the swampy woods, both kinglets, Yellow-rumped Warblers, Purple Finches (often present as well during their push north in April and early May), and occasional Red-breasted Nuthatches and Pine Siskins. In brushy clearings, look for sparrows: Fox, Field, White-crowned, American Tree, and other goodies.

In late spring and summer, common woodland breeders include Red-eyed Vireo, Great Crested Flycatcher, Scarlet Tanager, Acadian Flycatcher, House Wren, Eastern Wood-Pewee, Northern Parula, and Wood Thrush. A pair or two of Kentucky Warblers and Louisiana Waterthrushes probably nest.

Two Main Trails: Two main trails meander along, or cross, the streams and woods. To explore the park and these trails fully, you will need a spirit of adventure. The park's paths are neither paved nor sufficiently wide. It is wise to take precautions against ticks and poison ivy. Multiflora rose and tall weeds dominate the open brushy areas and open woods; if you leave the wide trail, expect to encounter thorns and burs. The north trail often requires a few stream crossings, making waterproof footwear the gear of choice. (Just think, many birders travel much farther to enjoy such a wilderness experience!)

South trail: From the far (south) end of the parking lot, a gravel path (often chained to bar vehicles) leads through a thin line of trees to a soccer field. (Check the hedges and young trees around this field for sparrows and interesting migrants.) From the far left corner of this field, a mown grass path—the south trail—leads down to a stream and a small wooden bridge (known as the Boy Scout Bridge, after its creators). The trail is perhaps a bit over a half-mile long and parallels the stream, finally ending by a wide, log-strewn bend in the stream. This area is often very birdy, good for Warbling Vireo in spring and early summer, and for woodpeckers, sparrows, and a variety of warblers in migration, including (for a few lucky souls) Mourning Warbler in mid to late May and September to early October. This part of the park may be altered, depending on the fate of the Inter-County Connector; it lies along the proposed Master Plan alignment.

The beginning of this path, from the soccer field to the bridge, is "newer" habitat. Its grasses and scattered young bushes often harbor good numbers of Field Sparrows and Dark-eyed Juncos, and should be investigated carefully for such possible rarities as Clay-colored Sparrow. The path, in places narrow but easily followed, continues into tall multiflora rose brambles favored by large numbers of sparrows. In addition to abundant White-throated and Song sparrows, these include White-crowned and Swamp, a Lincoln's Sparrow or two in May, September, or early October, and—especially in November and March—a few Fox Sparrows. In spring and early summer, look for Yellow-breasted Chats in the brambles and young trees.

North trail: The north trail leads from the left-hand parking spots nearest the park entrance along a paved path and bridge that cross the spindly stream. The vegetation around the stream and the field edge pulses with morning activity, led by American Goldfinches, Eastern Kingbirds, Eastern Phoebes, Song Sparrows, and Eastern Bluebirds. The bridge leads to a soccer field; follow the right side of the playing field to the far right corner. From there, a mowed path leads into woods and hedge to the right. During warbler migration, the first 100 or so yards of this trail can be very productive, as the

Clay-colored Sparrow

first sun warms the tops of the trees. But don't forget to scan mid-level or low bushes and branches for Mourning or Wilson's warblers among the many Common Yellowthroats. The path soon approaches the stream. Along this first stretch, open field and thicket predomi-nate on the left, while tangled woodland edge, with scattered dead trees, lines the stream bank on the right. This spot is often good for woodpeckers. Of the seven local species, only Red-headed Wood-pecker is rare in the park.

The trail continues to the left, passing a swampy thicket on the left (with the stream close by on the right). In spring, this area has pro-duced Mourning, Golden-winged, and migrating Kentucky war-blers, as well as Northern Waterthrush. A bit farther on, the trail again becomes open on the left and wooded on the right. When the wild grape tangles on the far left are ripe (late summer/early fall), you may find flocks of American Robins and Cedar Waxwings joined by any of the brown-backed thrushes. At the end of the clear-ing, the path jogs right and appears to end at a washed-out old road. A few steps after the turn, but before the stream, a narrow trail on the left side cuts up to the edge of the golf course. Prairie Warblers sing and likely nest along the rough edges of the fairways.

Returning to the main path, you now face your first stream crossing. The stream here can be gushing or almost dry, depending upon the weather. Taking care not to fall, try to cross the stream bed. Straight ahead the old roadbed, now overgrown, continues into mature secondary deciduous forest bordered by swampy spots. Be prepared to climb over or walk around a few fallen trees that cross the path. In migration, this stretch is particularly good for migrating thrushes, Northern Waterthrush, Black-throated Blue Warbler, and sometimes Lincoln's Sparrow. Kentucky Warbler and Louisiana Waterthrush often sing from deep in the woods on the right; both have probably nested there.

Toward the backstretch of this leg of the path, a stand of skeletal dead oaks (probably casualties of earlier gypsy moth infestation) skirts the trail. Pileated and other woodpeckers, White-breasted Nuthatch, and chickadee/titmouse flocks frequent this area, and sometimes an accipiter perches in the trees. The intrepid birder who continues down the trail past these trees soon reaches a second, wider stream crossing. You usually need to wade to get across, but your compensation is that, immediately up a small rise, you reach an old construction clearing that provides an open habitat far different from the shady, woodsy one you just traversed. No permanent trail exists in this park clearing, so that if you continue, you must bushwhack through hip-high goldenrod, thistle, and multiflora rose, keeping the woods to your right.

The fenced drainage pools and grassy open area bordered by hedges and woods are often productive for all three mimids, both orioles, Willow Flycatcher (in late May and early summer around the drainage pool willows), Yellow Warbler, Green Heron, Red-winged Blackbird, and flyover hawks, swallows, and Great Blue Herons. In winter, sparrows, including Fox, are drawn to the brambles. Until recently, Northern Bobwhites and an Eastern Meadowlark or two inhabited this area; they may turn up again.

You are now at the edge of Northwest Branch Park and should take care not to trespass on the adjacent farm. (Far to the right, the back end of the Trolley Museum is visible.) From the clearing, narrow forest trails—mainly deer paths obstructed here and there by thorns and poison ivy—lead back to Layhill Park's playing fields. It's easy to get lost here, though the woods are not extensive. First-time visitors should probably backtrack and take the long, tried-and-true way back to the parking lot. Ɏ

—Howard Youth

Black-and-white Warbler

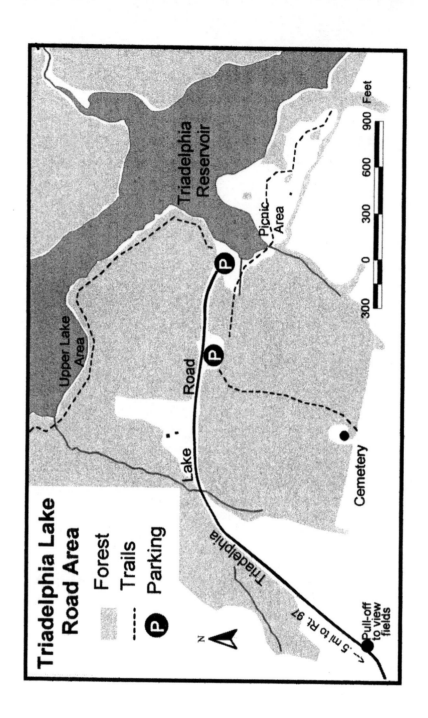

Triadelphia Lake
Road Area

Forest
Trails
P Parking

N

Triadelphia Reservoir

Upper Lake
Area

Road

Picnic
Area

Lake

Cemetery

Triadelphia

.5 mi to Rt. 97

Pull-off
to view
fields

300   0   300   600   900 Feet

Triadelphia Lake Road, Sunshine

Triadelphia Lake is a large body of water at the upper end of Triadelphia Reservoir, where the Patuxent River joins the Cattail River between Howard and Montgomery counties. The Triadelphia Lake area consists mainly of second-growth deciduous woods around the water, with a mowed picnic area set beneath a few large old oak trees, and some surrounding hedgerow as well. Fields along the top of Triadelphia Lake Road, which are leased to local farmers by the Washington Suburban Sanitary Commission (WSSC), are usually planted in grasses. Along the margins of these fields are shrubby areas attractive to various warblers, vireos, and sparrows.

Directions: From I-495, take exit 31A, Georgia Avenue (Route 97), and drive 15.5 miles north to the junction with New Hampshire Avenue (Route 650) in the town of Sunshine. Head north on Georgia 0.5 mile to the first right turn, Triadelphia Lake Road.

The area: Parking is provided in a paved lot (the main lot) at the water's edge, which also has a boat-launching ramp.

Another, more centrally located gravel lot is provided for overflow parking. The best birding occurs here from dawn to around noon, particularly in spring and autumn migrations, though summer and winter certainly have interesting bird life. A day in early May could produce 100 species, but 65 to 70 is more likely, even with an early start.

Site at a Glance

Triadelphia

Best birds:
Waterfowl, shorebirds/waders, thrushes/forest species, vireos/warblers, sparrows

Habitat:
Deciduous woods, open water, upland fields

Conditions:
Mostly easy walking on well-maintained trails or on roadways with little traffic

Best seasons:
Late winter through early summer; late summer through early autumn

Amenities:
Portable toilets in parking lot; general store (food, gas) 1/2 mile south

The fields on both sides of the road, as well as all the wooded land you will be birding, are owned and maintained by the WSSC. Please respect their property and the "No Trespassing" signs and stay on marked trails, the roadway, or the picnic area. A metal security gate located 0.7 mile from Georgia Avenue opens and closes automatically an hour before dawn and an hour after dusk. WSSC security personnel regularly patrol the property in blue vehicles. Please report any suspicious activity to the Brighton Dam Information Center, a cabin located on Brighton Dam Road (see Four Gems map), at 301–774–9124. Maps of the reservoir and an environmental education information sheet are available at the cabin.

Suggested routes: Begin at the fields along the road. Stop at the first locked gate on your right, about 0.2 mile from Georgia Avenue. Park as far off the road as possible (use your hazard flashers). A scope is helpful here to scan the fields, which slope away into the distance. In spring migration, any upland species is possible. The regulars include Northern Bobwhite, Eastern Meadowlark, Eastern Kingbird, Brown Thrasher, Northern Mockingbird, Gray Catbird, Indigo Bunting, Grasshopper and Field sparrows, swallows, Chimney Swift, Red-winged Blackbird, hawks and falcons, and flyover long-legged waders. The first two weeks in May produce good numbers of Bobolinks and sometimes a calling Ring-necked Pheasant (though seeing one is unlikely).

After spending some time here, continue driving down the road with your windows open, in season, to listen for bird songs. Park in the gravel (overflow) lot on your right. Parking here allows you to return to your vehicle at least twice to drop off or pick up extra clothing, bug spray, or a forgotten field guide. Begin by looking and listening for birds from the gravel lot. The area surrounding the lot is attractive to warblers and vireos, tanagers and buntings, and a good place to scan for flyovers.

The Cemetery Trail (marked by a brown sign) heads out from the southwest corner of the lot. This short trail (less than 0.25 mile) leads slightly uphill through second-growth deciduous woods and ends at a small cemetery where you will have another view, from a different angle, of the agricultural fields that you scanned previously from the road. The woods can be quiet or birdy, depending on the season and

MOB '98   *Bobolink*

the vagaries of the weather. Butterflies seem to like the open, sunny areas of woods near the top of the trail. Hiking quietly along here one morning, I surprised a Barred Owl sitting in a tree, being dive-bombed by a pair of gnatcatchers! Another time, a Worm-eating Warbler fed in some dead leaves hanging in a tree only 15 feet away, oblivious to my presence.

Other good finds along here include Blue-headed Vireo as well as Brewster's, Black-throated Blue, Black-and-white, and Blue-winged warblers (nests at top of hill). Ovenbird and American Redstart nest here too. You may find Yellow-breasted Chat, Yellow-billed Cuckoo, thrushes, woodpeckers, and Rose-breasted Grosbeak. Give yourself at least one hour for this trail and then retrace your steps to the gravel parking lot.

A second trail (also marked by a brown sign) heads down to the reservoir from the gravel lot's southeast corner. This trail winds its way to the picnic area and provides a completely different habitat. Both orioles, Eastern Bluebird, American Goldfinch, and Eastern Phoebe are all easy to find here in season, as are Chipping and Field sparrows, Prairie Warbler, Yellow-throated, Red-eyed, and White-eyed vireos, woodpeckers, and wrens. Scanning the reservoir could yield almost anything, from waders to shorebirds, from loon to Osprey, as well as Belted Kingfisher, Cliff Swallow, either species of vulture, Bald Eagle (a pair nests on the reservoir) and, in late April and September, kettling Broad-winged Hawks. A recent May Count discovered a pair of Golden-winged Warblers in the picnic area. Spend at least one-and-a-half to two hours here, giving yourself time to fully explore the shrubby edge habitat beyond the picnic grounds. Take the same trail back as far as the main parking lot.

A third trail begins at the northwest corner of the main parking lot, where the boat ramp is located. Climb the small wooden steps (known as the Boy Scout steps for the scout who built them as part of his Eagle project) cut into the hillside and hike through the woods along the reservoir. This trail winds through a variety of wooded habitats and eventually comes out at Patuxent River State Park on Route 97 near the Howard County line. Walk as far as time allows, at least as far as the upper lake area of the reservoir, where the trail gradually turns left. A few short trails leading off the right side of the main trail will take you through the woods down to the water's edge. Pine Warblers frequent the pines at the beginning of the trail, Yellow-bellied Sapsuckers are found in March and April, and any warbler might show up in migration (listen especially for Worm-eating). Ducks and waders, as well as shorebirds, gulls, and Caspian Terns, are possible at the right season. A Tricolored Heron was found here once, and Wild Turkeys like the wooded hillsides. I once saw three river otters cavorting in the waters here, and early spring wildflowers are both plentiful and beautiful. Allow an hour or two on this trail, then retrace your steps to the main parking lot.

Finally, for your fourth hike, walk up Triadelphia Lake Road back to the fields where you started, birding up one side and down the other. This is what I like to call "the birdiest mile in Montgomery County" (counting about half a mile each way). You'll walk through a wide variety of habitats: the water and its surrounding woods, grassy areas next to a small stream, mixed evergreen/deciduous woods where Great Horned Owls nest, second-growth scrubby areas and, finally, the agricultural fields at the top of the hill. Warblers, vireos, tanagers, and sparrows (including lots of towhees) are all here; in summer, a male Ruby-throated Hummingbird frequently perches on dead snags near the small bridge. Woodpeckers of all species except Red-headed can be found here, and a nice variety of butterflies as well.

When it's 95 degrees and horribly hot, it can be 10 degrees cooler along this road, and a breeze almost always blows down the hill. It is also very quiet, with just a handful of cars (mostly fishermen) driving past on a weekend morning, so you can generally walk in the center of the roadway. (Watch for vehicles, however.) Where else in Montgomery County can you do this? Regulars include White-eyed Vireo, Yellow-breasted Chat, Blue-winged Warbler, Common Yellowthroat, Indigo Bunting, Eastern Towhee, and Acadian, Great Crested, and occasionally Willow flycatchers. Kentucky and Hooded warblers are possible, as are thrushes, both orioles, American Kestrel, and other flyover hawks.

From May to the end of summer, the gated field on the north side of the road at the top of the hill usually holds at least a pair of Grasshopper Sparrows. The male can often be found singing from the white survey posts in the center of a scrubby area across from the gate. Have patience and use a scope for really great views of this declining (in the East) species.

Recent good finds here include a singing male Dickcissel and a female Blue Grosbeak, both in late spring/early summer of 1998, and in May 1999 a first-spring male Blue Grosbeak. Allow at least an hour, more likely two, for this part of the walk.

Obviously the walk I have outlined would take more than half a day. Pack a picnic lunch and make a day of it, or do two of the trails on Saturday and the other two on Sunday. Spring and fall migrations are the best times, but try it at any season. Y

—*Rick Sussman*

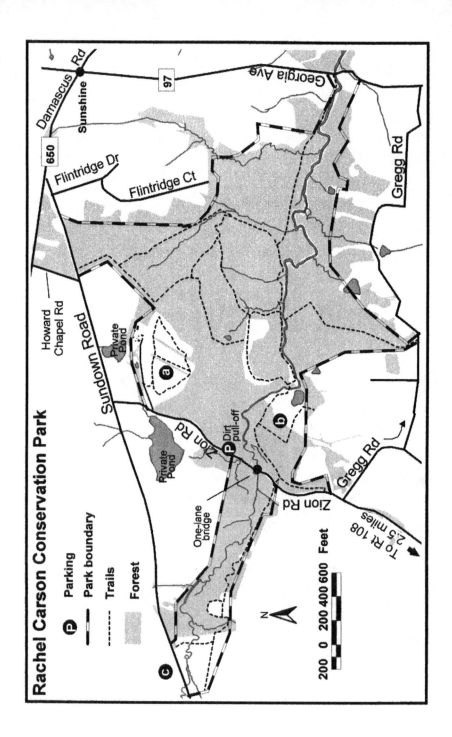

Rachel Carson Conservation Park

P Parking

Park boundary

Trails

Forest

200 0 200 400 600 Feet

N

To Rt 108 2.5 miles

Rachel Carson Conservation Park, Sunshine

I t is fitting that this park was named for biologist and author Rachel Carson (1907–64) who wrote her final and most influential work, *Silent Spring*, here in Montgomery County. Published in 1962, the book sounded an environmental clarion call that ultimately resulted in the founding of the Environmental Protection Agency, the banning of DDT, and the passage of other significant environmental legislation. A long-time county resident, Rachel Carson left a portion of her property wild—as she stated in a letter to a friend—"for the birds and frogs."

M-NCPPC and Montgomery County Parks designated this 648-acre tract as a conservation park on two accounts: first, to preserve its exemplary natural communities and populations of rare plants and animals, and second, to protect its unique archeological and historical resources. The park thus offers a wide variety of natural habitats and historical sites for birders, naturalists, and history buffs alike to explore.

Within the park are some of the most important stands of mature upland chestnut oak forest in the Mid-Atlantic states, as well as rich bottomland forests, old fields, hedgerows, small ponds, and the picturesque Hawlings River. The large quartz outcrops in the park provided early Native Americans with a source of raw material for stone tools. These same rock outcrops were later used as hiding spots by slaves fleeing north via the Underground Railroad. The

Rachel Carson

Best birds:
Thrushes/forest species, sparrows

Habitat:
Woods, fields, stream, small pond

Conditions:
Trails muddy in wet weather

Best seasons:
Spring and fall migration

Amenities:
None

Hawlings River was once the source of power for two mills. Remnants of the earliest—in operation from 1769 to 1900—can be found east of Zion Road; a second mill, just west of Georgia Avenue, operated from 1840 to 1926, and parts of the old dam are still visible.

The park is currently undeveloped, and the only amenity is a sometimes bewildering network of unmarked trails. Development of a more refined trail system and parking area is scheduled to begin in 2001 but may not be completed for a year or two. Until then, be prepared for trails that are generally good, but can be muddy after rains. Rubber boots can be helpful in crossing the stream, as there are no bridges and the Hawlings River is just wide enough to make a dry crossing difficult without them. Also, be aware that as development proceeds, temporary parking areas and trails may be shifted around, but signs should direct visitors to new areas and trails.

Directions: From I-495, take exit 31A, Georgia Avenue (Route 97), drive north 10.3 miles to the town of Olney, and turn left onto Route 108. Continue approximately 2.5 miles and turn right onto Zion Road. Proceed 2.6 miles and cross a one-lane bridge, keeping alert for fast-moving cars. In about 200 yards, turn onto the small dirt pull-off on the right and park. Until the park is developed, this is the only safe and legal parking area. Suggested walks begin at this point.

From I-270, take exit 8, Shady Grove Road, east. Proceed 3.5 miles and turn right onto Muncaster Mill Road. At 0.25 mile, turn left onto Muncaster Road. Go 3.5 miles to the end of Muncaster Road and turn right onto Route 108. In less than 50 yards, turn left onto Brookville Road. Drive 0.5 mile to the first stop sign, Zion Road, and turn left. Proceed 2.1 miles to a one-lane bridge, and follow directions as above.

Area (a): A good place to start birding Rachel Carson Park is the area of old fields, hedgerows, and wood edges off Zion Road, designated (a) on the map. This will eventually be the entrance to the park but is now marked with "No Parking" signs, so you will have to walk. From the parking area described above, bird your way north up Zion Road toward Sundown Road approximately a quarter mile to the gravel driveway on the right. Follow the driveway, birding the

Scarlet Tanager

open areas along the mowed paths. Mixed habitats offer good bird-ing throughout the year. Common spring and summer species include Eastern Phoebe, Great Crested Flycatcher, Eastern Bluebird, Gray Catbird, Northern Mockingbird, Brown Thrasher, Eastern Towhee, Indigo Bunting, Red-winged Blackbird, and Baltimore Oriole. Look over the open fields for soaring Red-tailed and Red-shouldered hawks and Black and Turkey vultures (all of which nest in the park). In fall and winter, walk along the wood edge and hedgerows looking for sparrows, including Field, Song, White-throated, and Dark-eyed Junco, as well as occasional American Tree, Fox, and White-crowned sparrows. The small stream and wet woods along the gravel driveway attract birds looking to bathe. The house at the end of the drive is a private residence; please maintain a respectful distance and do not enter the mowed yard. Trails will eventually lead from this site to the rest of the park, but until they are constructed, it is best to backtrack to your car after birding the area.

Most of the park trails go through mature woods, and a number of circular walks are possible (see map). Like most woods, they are best in the morning. All the common forest birds can be found here. In drier upland areas, watch for Great Crested Flycatcher, Red-eyed Vireo, Ovenbird, Worm-eating Warbler, and Scarlet Tanager. Along streams and bottomlands, expect Wood Thrush and Louisiana Waterthrush. Common species throughout the forested areas include Eastern Wood-Pewee, Acadian Flycatcher, and Pileated, Hairy, Downy, and Red-bellied woodpeckers, as well as Northern Flicker and White-breasted Nuthatch.

An additional attraction for birders is the large pond visible from Zion Road adjacent to the park. This pond is on private property and should be viewed from the roadside and only from outside the fence. The waterfowl-watching opportunities are covered in more detail in the Duck Ponds site description.

Area (b): My favorite walk is about 1.5 miles round trip and can take one-and-a-half to two hours, depending on what you find. From the parking area, walk south on Zion Road for about a quarter mile. The birding along the road can be very good, but exercise caution on this fast-moving, winding road. (Traffic is generally heavy during week-day commuting hours and light on weekend mornings.) About 150 yards beyond the one-lane bridge, take the trail to the left. It winds uphill through second growth and then down through open woods, good for Eastern Wood-Pewee, Great Crested and Acadian flycatchers, Wood Thrush, Ovenbird, and an occasional Northern Parula.

After about a third of a mile, the forest opens into a secluded area of old field, wetland swamp, and a small lily-covered pond—one of the best wildlife-watching places I've ever found. The overgrown field will likely produce Yellow-breasted Chat, Common Yellowthroat, Field Sparrow, Eastern Towhee, and Indigo Bunting. As you approach the pond, you may flush a Belted Kingfisher or Green or Great Blue herons. A pair or two of Mallards and Canada Geese nest here each year. Despite the pond's small size, you could scare up a Common Goldeneye, Hooded Merganser, or Ring-necked Duck from late fall to early spring. This is a great place to linger a while and see what comes to you. A visit to the pond and adjacent stream just before dusk will likely offer views of beaver, muskrat, and (if you're really lucky) a mink or even a river otter. River otter scat—about a half inch in diameter and composed of fish scales and crayfish parts—can usually be found along the pond edge. If you walk out at dusk, don't be surprised to see an owl cross your path; Great Horned, Barred, and Screech owls all nest here.

Area (c): An additional spot worth checking is near the Hawlings River Bridge on Sundown Road. From the parking area, drive north on Zion Road to the intersection with Sundown, turn left, and proceed about a mile to the bridge. Park just past the bridge, being careful to pull as far off the road as possible (people like to drive fast here too!) The old field and tree-lined stream on the south side of the road is park property. There are no trails, but the overgrown field area is accessible by walking back up the road about 150 yards. This is a good spot to find Willow Flycatcher, Belted Kingfisher, Yellow-throated Vireo, Yellow Warbler, and Grasshopper Sparrow. The north side of Sundown Road is private property. The many dead trees on the far woods edge are worth scanning for woodpeckers; Red-headed Woodpeckers were observed here several times in early summer of 2000. Y

—Rob Gibbs

LITTLE
TREASURES

Ruby-throated Hummingbird

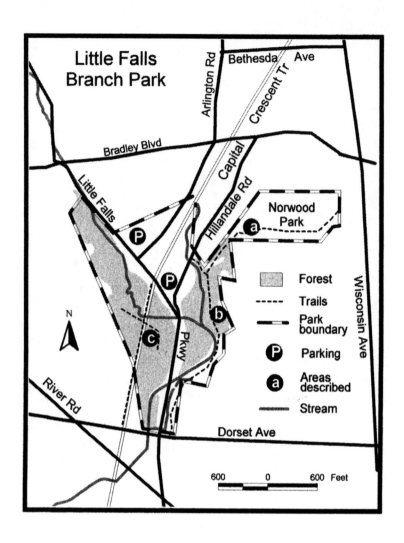

Little Falls
Branch Park

Arlington Rd

Bethesda Ave

Crescent Tr

Bradley Blvd

Little Falls

Capital

Hillandale Rd

Norwood
Park

ⓐ

P

P

ⓑ

Forest

Trails

Park
boundary

P Parking

ⓐ Areas
described

Stream

Wisconsin Ave

ⓒ

Pkwy

River Rd

Dorset Ave

600   0   600 Feet

N

Little Falls Branch Park, Bethesda

F or the growing townhouse and condominium population of central Bethesda, or for anyone in this part of the county who wants to get in an hour of birding en route to a downtown job, this section of parkland along Little Falls Parkway between Bradley Boulevard and Dorset Avenue offers a nice variety of habitat. Here, in a relatively small and compact area, you will find a mix of open parkland, ball fields, hedgerows, overgrown areas, mostly channelized streamside with large shade trees, and several acres of remnant second-growth deciduous forest. Migration periods offer the best opportunities. Because of heavy local traffic and the popularity of the Bethesda Pool and the Capital Crescent Trail on weekends, this area is best visited during the week and in the early morning hours.

Directions: From I-495, take exit 39, River Road, east towards DC approximately 4 miles. Shortly after passing under the Capital Crescent trail hiker-biker bridge, you will come to Little Falls Parkway; turn left.

From northwest DC, take River Road west 0.7 mile beyond Western Avenue. The second light is Little Falls Parkway; turn right.

There is free parking in two lots along the right (east) side of Little Falls Parkway, one just north of Arlington Road and another (smaller) one at the Bethesda Pool at Hillandale Road. There are no public toilet facilities.

Suggested routes: Three general areas are worth exploring (see map):

Areas (a) and (b) are both reached from the Bethesda Pool lot by walking a short distance up Hillandale Road and crossing (carefully —traffic is swift and unforgiving here) into the park on a well-marked paved trail. Area (c) is reached by joining the Capital Crescent trail where it crosses Little Falls Parkway.

Area (a): Soon after you enter the park from Hillandale Road, a path leads to the left, heading up into Norwood Park. (Going straight leads to Area (b), described below.) The park itself is mowed so short and is so open that it attracts few birds, but Killdeer is possible and the edges and shrubby middle hold sparrows (sometimes including Swamp) and the usual resident passerines and woodpeckers. The cedars and white pines along the east edge of the park are sometimes good for wintering small birds. Hawks fly over in migration, and a Red-shouldered Hawk seen frequently may be a local nester. Baltimore Oriole and Rose-breasted Grosbeak are regular in migration. Gray Catbirds are numerous in spring and summer, and Brown Thrasher is occasionally seen. The piece of Area (a) closest to the main trail merits wandering off the pavement if it's dry enough. "Spishing" in the brambles and overgrown tangles may produce White-eyed Vireo, among others.

Area (b): The main trail runs south from Hillandale Road, just east of and alongside the channelized stream. The trail is paved, but off the trail it is often wet and muddy. There are lots of big shade trees and an abundance of smaller trees and thickets. On a still, early May morning, the stretch between Hillandale and Dorset Avenue can be

White-eyed Vireo

full of migrants; foggy, overcast weather seems particularly good. In 20-plus years of occasional birding here, I have identified 21 species of warblers, the most common being Blue-winged, Yellow, Black-throated Green, American Redstart, and Common Yellowthroat. Northern Waterthrush is a regular migrant in May; listen for its loud, ringing song. Louisiana Waterthrush has been spotted here too, but no longer breeds. Mallards are often seen in the concreted "stream," depending on water depth. Wood Duck and Solitary Sandpiper are occasionally found. There should be an Eastern Phoebe nest somewhere nearby; listen for Eastern Wood-Pewees and Great Crested Flycatchers here or over the road in Area (c). At Dorset Avenue you can turn around and retrace your steps, or cross Little Falls Parkway and return via the Capital Crescent Trail within Area (c).

Area (c): The stretch of the Capital Crescent Trail west of Little Falls Parkway in the direction of River Road was formerly an overgrown railroad right-of-way and used to be better for birding than it is now. However, it is flanked on the south by a nice patch of oak–beech–tulip poplar woodland, and a short trail runs into the woods on the west, beginning just after the stream crossing. Look for Scarlet Tanager high in the trees in the woodland area and for Ovenbird low down; both species may have bred here in the past. Another very short trail on the opposite side of the Crescent Trail gives a view over the stream into a wet area noted for its Common Yellowthroats. House and Carolina wrens should be audible and visible in this vicinity. Watch for fast-moving bikers and rollerbladers at all times of the day and night! Ɏ

—*Michael Bowen*

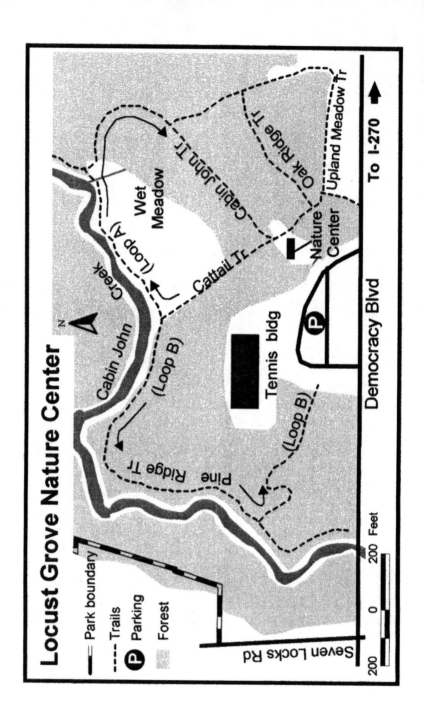

Locust Grove Nature Center

Park boundary
Trails
Parking
Forest

To I-270

Democracy Blvd

Seven Locks Rd

200   0   200 Feet

Nature Center

Upland Meadow Tr

Oak Ridge Tr

Cabin John Tr

Wet Meadow

(Loop A)

Cattail Tr

Cabin John Creek

(Loop B)

Pine Ridge Tr

(Loop B)

Tennis bldg

N

Locust Grove Nature Center, Bethesda

P art of the 545-acre Cabin John Regional Park, Locust Grove Nature Center and its surrounding trails offer a surprising diversity of habitat for the birder with a free hour or two. Smack in the heart of suburbia, this tranquil, woodsy setting is graced with a gently flowing creek whose eroded banks have provided nesting cavities for Belted Kingfishers. Over the years, observers have recorded 122 species of birds, and breeding bird surveys for the past six years have listed 57 species, including Yellow-billed Cuckoo, Pileated Woodpecker, White-breasted Nuthatch, Louisiana Water-thrush, Common Yellowthroat, and Indigo Bunting.

Directions: Heading east on I-495 from the Potomac River, take the I-270 spur north, toward Rockville, and exit at Democracy Boulevard west. Follow Democracy Boulevard past the large shopping mall and across Westlake Drive; in another 0.4 mile you will come to the Cabin John Park entrance on the right. Parking is plentiful.

Heading west on I-495, take exit 36, Old Georgetown Road. Drive north 0.8 mile to Democracy Boulevard, turn left, and drive 1.8 miles to the Cabin John Park entrance on the right.

The area: Trails are open daily from sunrise to sunset. Locust Grove Nature Center (reached by crossing a wooden bridge at the northeast edge of the lot) is open year-round (except holidays) Tuesday–Saturday from 9 a.m. to 5 p.m. Inside the center you will find trail maps, species lists, and bathrooms. The center offers a number of diverse nature programs for adults and children. Call 301–299–1990 for more information.

The 40 acres surrounding the center include dry and wet meadow, woodland edge and thickets, and both upland and floodplain forest. Within these varied habitats and around the center itself, you should find birds in all seasons. During spring and fall migration, a short walk could yield any of the following warblers: Yellow, Black-throated Blue, Black-and-white, Blackpoll, Ovenbird, and American Redstart. While enjoying lunch at the center's picnic tables on a fine summer day, you might also satisfy your birding appetite with sightings of Ruby-throated Hummingbird, House Wren, Eastern Bluebird (they nest in the dry meadow near the parking lot), and Indigo Bunting. In winter, it's always worth checking the well-stocked feeders and the pond near the observation deck for resident woodpeckers, American Goldfinch, White-throated Sparrow, and (infrequently) Red-breasted Nuthatch and Fox Sparrow.

Suggested routes: For an early morning stroll or a lunchtime break, two well-marked half-mile loops (Loop A and Loop B) offer good birding rewards with generally easy walking and only a few modest uphill stretches. While each loop can easily be done in under an hour, there are plenty of options if you want to wander further. Both loops begin behind the Nature Center, and both start on the green-blazed Cattail Trail (may be renamed in the near future).

Loop A follows the Cattail Trail down a series of wide "steps" to a large meadow on the right. Keep moving right, following the green markers as the trail skirts the meadow. The wet meadow, with two magnificent sycamores (often decorated with Eastern Bluebirds), can be productive in all seasons. On your left, Cabin John Creek may yield Great Blue and Green herons in season. The brambly tangle between the path and the creek is good for expected edge species—Northern Mockingbird, Northern Cardinal—as well as Common Yellowthroat and Northern Parula. Look out in the meadow itself for Field and other sparrows. Red-shouldered Hawks and Pileated Woodpeckers have nested in nearby trees across the creek. At the meadow's end, the green trail intersects the blue-blazed Cabin John Trail. Turn right (following signs toward the center) and continue moving uphill following the blazes through a forest of oak and hickory. When the path dips into a hollow and comes to a second small footbridge, take a moment to marvel at the century-old "Grandaddy" tulip poplar on the right and to listen for the reliable Acadian Flycatcher. As you head back to the center, check the woods in spring for Red-eyed and other vireos and thrushes and in winter for woodpeckers and Yellow-rumped Warbler.

Loop B also begins on the Cattail Trail, but upon reaching the large laminated park map, continue straight ahead rather than turning right as above. Currently called Pine Ridge, this orange-blazed trail may become a section of the Cabin John Trail in the future. The path takes you through an attractive floodplain forest along the Cabin John Creek. Listen on your right for the Belted Kingfisher's rattle. In spring, look and listen for Acadian Flycatcher, Wood Thrush, Northern Parula, and Ovenbird. When the trail forks, turn left and continue uphill. Here an old pine stand has given way to tulip poplar, oak, and beech. In winter, expect the usual woodland birds as you follow this pretty walk back to the parking lot.

Other trails: The blue-blazed trails at the Nature Center are just a small part of the nine-mile Cabin John Trail that begins on Mac-Arthur Boulevard near the old aqueduct bridge, follows the Cabin John stream valley, and ends several miles north of Locust Grove. If you follow the blue-blazed trail north (away from the center), you will eventually reach a part of the park that borders on a powerline cut. When you reach this open area, be sure to scan the brushy tangle and woodland edge on both sides of the cut for Gray Catbird, Brown Thrasher, Common Yellowthroat, Eastern Towhee, sparrows, and Indigo Bunting. Look for Cedar Waxwings in the deciduous trees on the north side of the powerline and check overhead for Red-tailed Hawks. Red-shouldered Hawks have nested in the lowland woods on the south side.

This area can also be accessed by driving to the park's athletic facilities (ball fields and skating rink) on Westlake Boulevard, about half a mile north of Democracy Boulevard. Turn left at the brown park sign and follow signs to Ball Field 3. In less than a quarter mile you will see a laminated map of the park trails on your right. Park in the lot opposite the sign and take the (unmarked) trail beside it. This short trail leads into the woods and soon meets the Cabin John Trail. Before you bear left to take up the trail as it parallels the cut, scan the open area for the edge birds and soaring raptors described above. By following the trail south for about 1.5 miles you could work your way back to the Nature Center, but you may opt instead to explore a shorter distance. In summer, take a few moments before returning to your car to scout the wood edge at the northwest side of the farthest parking lot (4) for Eastern Wood-Pewee, Great Crested Flycatcher, Red-eyed Vireo, Wood Thrush, and Ovenbird. Ỿ

—*Linda Friedland*

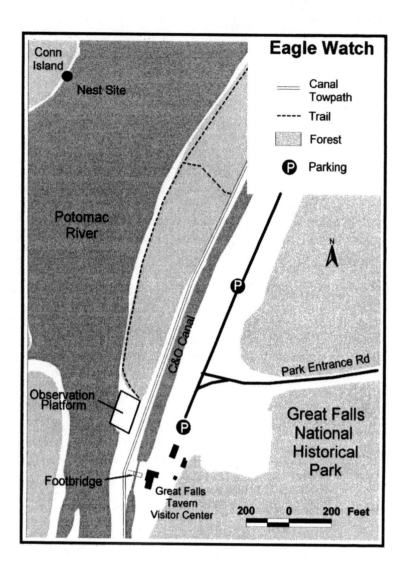

Eagle Watch

Canal Towpath
Trail
Forest
Parking

Conn Island
Nest Site
Potomac River
C&O Canal
Park Entrance Rd
Observation Platform
Footbridge
Great Falls Tavern Visitor Center
Great Falls National Historical Park

N

200 0 200 Feet

Bald Eagle Watch, Great Falls

A Bald Eagle soaring over the Potomac River is, happily, no longer an unusual sight in the National Capital area. But here in Montgomery County, birders have the rare opportunity to observe these magnificent birds throughout courtship and mating, nest building, incubation, and the rearing of chicks. Every year since 1986, a pair of Bald Eagles has nested on an island near the observation deck at Great Falls. The nest is the only known active Bald Eagle nest in Montgomery County and one of the furthest west of all documented nests in Maryland.

Directions: Use the directions provided in the C&O Canal section of this guide to reach Great Falls. Cross the footbridge over the canal, turn right onto the towpath, and continue about 25 yards to the concrete observation platform on your left. Looking out over the Potomac River you will see, just above the spillway, the half-mile-long Conn Island about 200 yards off the Maryland shore. The best place to observe the nest from the platform is from the extreme south (downstream) end. Scan the Conn Island shoreline going upstream until large trees near the platform block your view. At this point you should see the nest some 50–60 feet up in a large sycamore. Viewing is best with a scope. Early weekday mornings (best light) or late afternoons (glorious sunsets) are ideal. For a closer view of the nest, take your scope and follow the narrow riverside trail (can be quite muddy after rains) that begins just north of the platform, walking upstream until you are opposite the nest tree.

Watching throughout the year: Both birds were raised in captivity and banded before release. The male has a band on his right leg, while the larger female's is on her left. If you keep returning to the site over time, you may, as a dedicated eagle watcher, begin to discern subtle behavioral differences between the sexes.

The nest, weighing over 500 pounds, is reused year after year but needs constant repair. Work on the nest begins as early as September and continues even after incubation. At any time throughout the day you may see both adults (but mainly the male) bring twigs and small branches to work into the nest. As the primary nest-builder, the male will actually spend more time on the nest prior to incubation than the female.

By late October or early November, the birds will begin perching, often for hours, near the nest or on the north (upstream) end of the island. Check the sky for circling birds and the river for fishing activity (ever the opportunistic feeders, the eagles will sometimes take ducks as well). Listen also for their thin, high cries. At sunset they will return to the nest tree to roost.

January is the prime time for observing mating activity; often the pair will vocalize softly and alternately while perched on the nest itself. The pair continues to perch (and often preen) for long periods of time at the north end of the island.

Eggs are laid in mid-February. Typically, there is a period of false incubation during which both birds take turns sitting on the nest at various times during the three to five days before the eggs are actually laid. The established hatching time is 35 days. A sure sign that the one to three eggs have been laid: there will always be one adult sitting deep in the nest. While male and female share incubation duties, it is almost always the female that stays on the nest during the night. During the incubation period, you may happen upon an "exchange"—one bird alights on the nest rim and moments later the other flies off to hunt.

The sight of both birds perching on the rim of the nest usually indicates hatching—sometime from mid- to late March. When you see the adults bringing food to the nest, there's no doubt the chicks have hatched! The early feeding schedule is intense: The adults may bring food to the nest hourly. At that point it is worth checking the nest often, for you will soon be rewarded with the sight of fluffy gray heads popping up over the rim. As the weeks go by, the fast-growing chicks, now dark brown with gray beaks, will perch awkwardly on the edge of the nest, pumping their wings in preparation for flight.

Not all hatchings are successful. Severe weather or unexplained phenomena can mean nest failure. When an only chick dies, the female abandons the nest immediately, although the male continues to eat his food at the nest. The pair will not attempt a second brood.

If all goes well, though, the full-sized and vigorous young will have fledged by early June. Look for them in the vicinity of the nest or, at times, on a small island slightly upstream of the nest. The adults will continue to feed them until they have mastered the art of fishing for themselves. Then, around the end of July, the young are suddenly gone, off to form new territories, and the cycle begins again.

Enjoy the birds but remember that even though the pair has nested in this location for many years, actions such as loud noises or large gestures still may disrupt their nesting activities. Υ

—*Linda Friedland*

Immature Bald Eagle   MOB '98

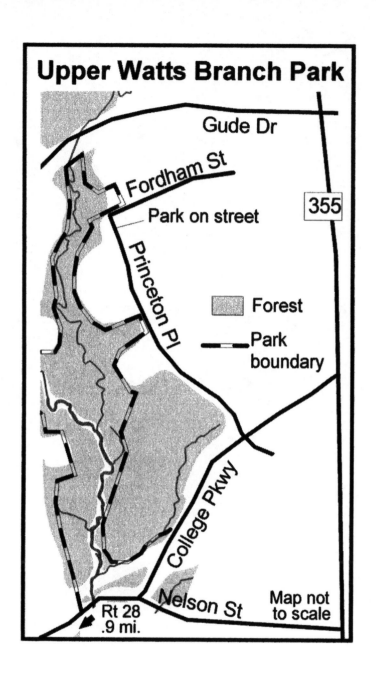

Upper Watts Branch Park

Gude Dr

Fordham St

Park on street

Princeton Pl

355

Forest

Park boundary

College Pkwy

Nelson St

Rt 28 .9 mi.

Map not to scale

Upper Watts Branch Park, Rockville  Site D

T his 55-acre park, which sits at the headwaters of Watts Branch, consists of mature beech, tulip poplar, and mixed oak with sycamore, green ash, and box elder in the floodplain. It is home to 43 species of breeding birds, with an additional 91 species using the habitat at different times of the year. Over 180 species have been seen in the immediate area. Of all the warblers regularly occurring in Maryland, only Swainson's Warbler has not been seen here. The park is situated between Woodley Gardens to the west and College Gardens to the east and is bounded by West Gude Drive to the north and Nelson Street to the south.

Directions: From I-270 northbound, take exit 6, West Montgomery Avenue (Route 28), staying in the left lane; this crosses West Montgomery Avenue and becomes Nelson Street. Proceed 0.9 mile to the third stop sign, College Parkway, and turn left. Go 0.4 mile to the stop sign at Princeton Place, turn left and proceed six blocks to a right turn where Princeton terminates and Fordham Street begins, and park.

From the southbound I-270 exit ramp, turn left (east) onto Route 28, cross over I-270, and turn left at the traffic light. Proceed as above.

From Route 355, turn onto College Parkway at College Plaza Shopping Center and proceed 0.4 mile to the second stop sign, Princeton Place. Turn right at Princeton Place and proceed six blocks (0.4 mile) to its termination at Fordham Street and park.

Suggested route: The most productive birding in both spring and fall migrations is along the edge of the woods bordering an open lot right at the intersection of Princeton and Fordham. Early morning is best, as the first sunlight bathes the edge and the migrants come out of the woods to feed on insects. The interior of the woods at this location is also productive, because of a permanent wetland fed by springs. Flycatchers, vireos, kinglets, mimids, warblers, tanagers, sparrows, orioles and finches are active on the edge of the woods, and hawks are frequently seen either overhead or emerging from a nighttime roost in the woods.

American Redstart

MOB '98

A path next to the last house on Princeton takes you directly (about 250 feet) to the bank of the stream and the path that parallels it. Excellent habitat for thrushes can be found by walking south (left) on the path about one block to the point at which the east slope of the valley opens up with mature trees and sparse understory. This habitat extends for about two more blocks. All of the eastern thrushes have been seen here; Gray-cheeked is usually present in mid- to late May.

Red-shouldered Hawks nest here and a Red-tailed Hawk is generally present in winter, along with the usual feeding flock of Carolina Chickadees, Tufted Titmice, White-breasted Nuthatches, American

Goldfinches, House Finches and woodpeckers (Red-bellied, Flicker, Downy, Hairy, and Pileated). Cardinals and White-throated Sparrows guard the entrance path at Fordham. Breeders include Ruby-throated Hummingbird, Eastern Wood-Pewee, Acadian and Great Crested flycatchers, Veery, Wood Thrush, Red-eyed Vireo and, sometimes, Kentucky Warbler.

To return to your car, retrace your steps. Y

—Paul J. O'Brien

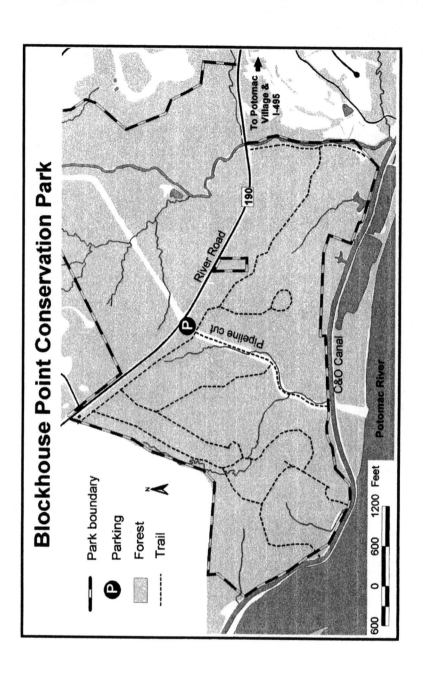

Blockhouse Point Conservation Park

Legend:
- Park boundary
- P Parking
- Forest
- Trail

N

To Potomac Village & I-495

190

River Road

Pipeline cut

C&O Canal

Potomac River

600 0 600 1200 Feet

Blockhouse Point
Conservation Park, Potomac

Blockhouse Point Conservation Park is named for the Civil War fortification built on a cliff that lies within its boundaries. The "blockhouse" served as an observation post and signal station for the Union forces patrolling the banks of the Potomac River. Situated between River Road and the C&O Canal, this 670-acre wooded tract, laced with several springs and streams, is a generally underbirded area. Aside from some initial traffic noise and the occasional distractions of dog-walkers or horse-riders, it can be a pleasant, productive place to spend an hour birding.

Directions: From I-495, take exit 39, River Road, toward Potomac. At 3.3 miles you will cross Falls Road; another 5.1 miles will bring you to Pennyfield Road. Continue another 1.2 miles and watch for a wooden fence on your left, marking the entrance to a gravel parking lot. It's easy to miss the unmarked lot on this curving, fast-paced road.

Suggested route: The parking lot (usually almost empty) has a kiosk with a map of the park's hiking and equestrian trails. Many of these trails can be birdy, but some are not particularly well marked and it's easy to lose your way (as I once did on a breeding bird survey).

A good alternative method of sampling the upland forest would be to take the equestrian trail just beyond the lot for a short distance, look and listen for woodland birds, and then return to the main path. The equestrian path on the right is a good choice, for the deciduous woods in spring often hold vireos, tanagers, and warblers while a stand of old pine (about 200 feet into the woods on the right) attracts mixed flocks of foraging winter birds.

If you have just an hour or so to bird, simply walk down the wide petroleum pipeline cut—a minuscule section of the 5,349-mile pipeline that begins in Texas and ends in New York—descending from the lot. This graveled roadway of some 2,500 feet leads directly to the canal but does not cross it, so there is no access to the towpath from this side.

On spring mornings, first check the large oaks and tulip poplars near the parking lot. As the sun hits the trees, you may find such delights as Pine and Palm warblers and other migrants. If you begin your walk in early April, you will almost certainly hear the ringing notes of a Louisiana Waterthrush along the creek that begins about a third of the way down the pipeline cut on the left. By early summer, the persistent buzzy trills of nesting Worm-eating Warblers coming from the upland woods on the right will tempt you to enter the woods in search of this voice-thrower.

Recent breeding bird surveys indicate the rich bird life in summer: Yellow-billed Cuckoo, Acadian Flycatcher, Red-eyed and Yellow-throated vireos, Wood Thrush, Northern Parula, Kentucky Warbler, Ovenbird, Scarlet Tanager, and Indigo Bunting. As summer progresses, you may have to be content with birding by ear.

In winter, large trees on both sides of the cut should hold most of the expected woodpeckers—Red-bellied, Yellow-bellied Sapsucker, Downy, Hairy, Northern Flicker, Pileated—as well as White-breasted Nuthatch, Brown Creeper, and Golden-crowned Kinglet. The grassy areas bordering the gravel path are usually mowed (and usually birdless), but piles of weathered logs and weedy patches close to the woods provide cover for Carolina Wren, Song and White-throated sparrows, and Dark-eyed Junco. As you continue along the cut and reach more level terrain, look above the creek on the left for a moss-covered rocky outcrop dotted with mountain laurel. A Winter Wren or two is likely to be nearby.

In all seasons, keep glancing skyward for raptors: This open expanse is good for spotting Broad-winged Hawk in spring and fall migration and Red-tailed Hawk and both vultures throughout the year. Infrequently, a Great Horned or Barred owl will put in a surprise appearance.

As you reach the end of the path and come to the canal, check the large white oak and smaller sycamores on the right, consistently good in spring for warblers (Cerulean is possible), tanagers, and orioles. Then look across the canal at the towpath; chances are you'll find fellow birders with binoculars focused on the very same birds. The "Blockhouse Point" cliff, where traces of the old fort remain, can be reached from here via the almost invisible path to your right, but it's a steep scramble and the path is often overgrown. Retrace your steps to the parking lot. ⅄

—*Linda Friedland*

Wood Thrush

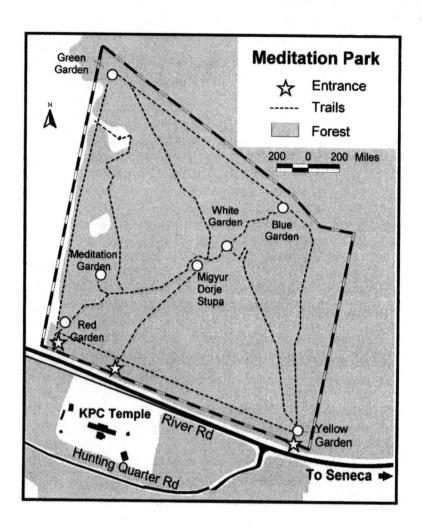

Meditation Park

☆ Entrance
------ Trails
▓ Forest

200 0 200 Miles

N

Green Garden

White Garden

Blue Garden

Meditation Garden

Migyur Dorje Stupa

Red Garden

KPC Temple

River Rd

Yellow Garden

Hunting Quarter Rd

To Seneca ➤

Meditation Park, Poolesville

Site F

One of the more unusual places to bird in Montgomery County, easily combined with a trip to Hughes Hollow or Riley's Lock, is the 65-acre Meditation Park across from the Kunzang Palyul Choling (KPC) Buddhist Temple on River Road in Poolesville. Two streams thread through the several miles of easy-to-medium walking trails (some steepish inclines). The park provides a good variety of habitats, from pasture and hedgerow scrub to fully mature hardwood forest. Along the trails, in addition to a broad selection of birds, you will find tranquil meditation gardens and the traditional Buddhist monuments called stupas. During hunting season especially, this beautiful site provides a welcome haven of peace. One of the resident monks has tallied 85 species over the course of several years.

> The temple is maintained for public use and is open 24 hours a day. Inside are trail maps, restrooms, and complimentary coffee or tea. Visitors are welcome to tour the beautiful shrine rooms. Signs say that it is necessary to obtain permission before entering the park, but birders are not required to do so.

Directions: From I-495, take exit 39, River Road (Route 190), toward Potomac. Drive west, through Potomac, 11.4 miles to a T-intersection and stop sign. Here River Road makes a left turn and is joined by Seneca Road (Route 112) from the right. Turn left and drive west on River Road for 3.5 miles. Just beyond Hunting Quarter Road, you will see the main Temple entrance on your left (18400 River Road). Park entrance to red garden is across road about 100 yards beyond Temple. Park either in main Temple parking lot or on side of road.

Suggested route: The "birdiest" trail is the half-mile walk that links the red and green gardens. This trail goes straight ahead as you enter the park and runs along the western boundary of the property. Along this section, look in the ground tangle and canopy of young trees for many of the 15 reported warbler species, including Wilson's, Canada, Bay-breasted, and Yellow-throated. Other spring and summer possibilities include Orchard Oriole, Rose-breasted and Blue grosbeaks, Great Crested Flycatcher, and Yellow-billed

Cuckoo (Black-billed was seen once). A little past the private residence and stable on the left (check for nesting Barn Swallows zipping in and out), a grove of trees gives way to pasture. Listen and look here for Yellow-breasted Chat, raptors, Field and White-crowned sparrows, and woodpeckers—all seven local species are possible. Just beyond the pasture the mature forest suddenly begins, with the higher canopy favored by Scarlet and Summer tanagers and warblers. Wood Thrush is likely here and, if you're really lucky, Wild Turkey.

Each year the stands of cedar on the property attract a large nesting population of Prairie Warblers, which start singing in April. The stream beds can produce Louisiana Waterthrush, Acadian Flycatcher, and Great Blue Heron. Wintertime is still active, with woodpeckers, both kinglets, Winter Wren, Cedar Waxwing, Brown Creeper, Barred Owl and, irregularly, Pine Siskin. Every year as the weather cools, dozens of Northern Rough-winged Swallows gather on the telephone wires at the temple entrance. Y

—*Konchog Norbu*

Black-billed Cuckoo

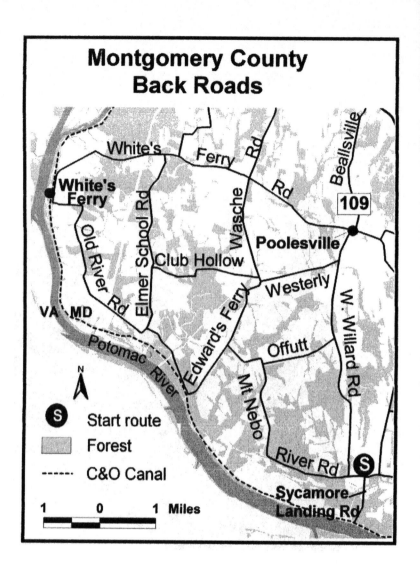

Montgomery County
Back Roads

White's
Ferry
Rd
Beallsville
White's
Ferry
109
Old River Rd
Elmer School Rd
Wasche
Club Hollow
Poolesville
Westerly
VA MD
W. Willard Rd
Potomac River
Edward's Ferry
Offutt
N
Mt Nebo
S Start route
Forest
------ C&O Canal
River Rd
S
Sycamore
Landing Rd
1   0   1 Miles

Back Roads, Western Montgomery County

Site G

The western portion of Montgomery County consists primarily of large tracts of forested and agricultural land. A series of paved and unpaved roads cross this area, running some 10.7 miles from the intersection of River Road and Sycamore Landing Road to White's Ferry. This route roughly parallels the Potomac River and the C&O Canal, although both are visible only at Edward's Ferry and White's Ferry.

The roads are easily navigated except in heavy rain or snow. Still, as you travel this route, there are a few precautions to keep in mind. First, although the primary road is River Road, its name changes several times on the way to White's Ferry before it eventually changes back to River Road. Second, the entire stretch is a series of narrow two-lane roads without convenient pull-offs, so when pulling over make sure that visibility is good in both directions. Finally, there are no facilities until you get to White's Ferry. However, armed with a full tank of gas, a scope, supplies of water and snacks, and a spirit of adventure, you should be rewarded with an enjoyable country ride and good birds. Western Montgomery County has also produced birds that are difficult to find elsewhere in the county: Sandhill Crane, Lapland Longspur, and Buff-breasted Sandpiper have all made appearances in recent years.

Suggested route:

0.0 miles: Set your trip odometer at the intersection of Sycamore Landing Road and River Road. (See McKee-Beshers WMA map.) Head west on River Road.

0.0 to 0.2 miles: In August and September check the telephone wires for Tree and Rough-winged swallows. The area at 0.2 miles can be productive for Bank Swallow.

1.75 miles: There is an entrance to a turf farm on your left; this is private property and should not be entered. Turn sharply right as River Road continues but changes its name to Mt. Nebo Road.

3.3 miles: Mt. Nebo swings left and becomes West Offutt Road.

3.8 miles: Start checking the fields on both sides of the road for Eastern Bluebird and the roadside weedy scrub for Savannah Sparrow.

4.25 miles: West Offutt dead-ends at a T-intersection and stop sign. Turn left onto Edward's Ferry Road. Approach this intersection slowly, on the lookout for accipiters (especially Cooper's Hawk) in nearby trees. Examine the nearby pine trees for Golden-crowned Kinglets. For the next mile, look for woodpeckers in the wooded area on your left, Red-tailed Hawks over the open fields, and swallows on the wires.

5.3 miles: There is a stop sign at a three-way intersection. Turn left at the "Park Entrance/Edward's Ferry" sign and park in the lot on the right. (Do not block the boat ramp.) Here you have access to the C&O Canal towpath, where you can take a short walk to look for seasonal specialties. In spring and early summer listen for flycatchers and warblers, in the winter months for Barred and Great Horned owls. Use your scope to scan the Potomac River for ducks, Osprey, eagles, and swallows. Exit Edward's Ferry and return to Edward's Ferry Road.

5.6 miles: Turn left. This is the fourth and final name change—welcome back to River Road! From here to White's Ferry, the road is unpaved and can be very dusty in dry weather. For the next half-mile, look and listen for American Redstart, Wood Thrush, and Wild Turkey in spring and summer. In winter, this stretch is good for Hermit Thrush.

6.3 miles: An underground gas line (marked above by poles) crosses the road. Check the secondary growth at the edges of the fields on both sides of the road for Eastern Towhee and Brown Thrasher. For the next mile, listen for American Woodcock, often heard "peenting" on warm evenings (especially those with a full moon) from mid-January to April.

6.7 miles: A one-lane bridge crosses over a creek.

Savannah Sparrow

7.0 miles: Turn left (still on River Road; Elmer School Road goes right), watching for small potholes for the next 0.1 mile.

7.1 miles: The road makes a 90-degree turn to the right; the Fairbanks Farm is on your left. During shorebird migration (March–May and July–August), if the field on your left is flooded, it can hold Least Sandpipers and both yellowlegs.

7.2 miles: The field on your right is good for displaying American Woodcock. Listen here for Great Horned Owl.

7.5 to 7.75 miles: Look in the small trees at the road's edge for winter sparrows, including White-crowned, White-throated, Fox (February and March) and American Tree.

7.75 miles to White's Ferry: The final three miles take you through an agricultural area that can be the most rewarding section of the trip in all seasons. On your left you will see the J.T. Patton Turf Farms; on your right are other private farm fields where crops rotate between corn and soybeans. Small wooded areas separate the crop fields. Both sides of the road are private property; do not enter the fields or farm driveways and do all birding strictly from the side of the road. The road is not heavily trafficked, but please park carefully, allowing room for other cars—and large trucks travelling to and from the turf farms—to pass.

7.75 to 8.75 miles: Scan the farm fields and the turf farm. During three weeks of July and August of 1995, a pair of Sandhill Cranes made daily visits to a soybean field on the right. Look for perched Red-tailed and Red-shouldered hawks along the tree lines and, during the summer months, American Kestrels on the power lines. Northern Harriers are possible from late August through May, especially over the fields on your right.

January to March is a good time to look for gulls; most of the time you will find Ring-billed, but an occasional Herring, Laughing, or Bonaparte's can show up in migration. Check the bushes and small trees at the edge of the road on your right for migrating Palm Warblers, as well as Savannah and Vesper sparrows.

The turf farm fields can be productive for shorebirds. Killdeer are likely almost any time (unless the winter is very cold or snowy). During migration you may find American Golden-Plover (September to November) as well as Pectoral Sandpiper (March to mid-May, and rarely, late July to October). Buff-breasted Sandpipers made an appearance in September 2000. During spring and fall migration, both Greater and Lesser yellowlegs and Least Sandpipers are likely.

From December to March, scope the turf farm fields for Horned Lark and American Pipit, especially after the fields have been plowed and manured. Lapland Longspur made an appearance in February 2001.

9.1 to 9.2 miles: Check the wooded areas for sparrows, Dark-eyed Junco, Eastern Towhee, and Brown Thrasher.

9.4 miles: A partially overgrown drive is on the right. During the summer months, check the edges of both sides of the drive for breeding White-eyed Vireo and Yellow-breasted Chat.

9.8 to 10.0 miles: Be on the lookout for a resident Red-tailed Hawk.

10.4 miles: River Road bends to the right and continues 0.3 mile to White's Ferry. Here you will find a small convenience store (open April to October), telephone, and portable toilets. Once again you can access the river (scan for Bald Eagles in winter) and the canal. And should you wish to continue your explorations into Virginia, a car ferry will transport you across the Potomac.

To return to "suburban" Montgomery County, you may either:

1) Continue on White's Ferry Road for approximately 6.5 miles to Poolesville; or

2) Retrace your steps to Sycamore Landing Road. Helpful hint: Following the directions outbound, including turning into Edward's Ferry, all of your turns were left-hand turns. On the way back, all of the turns will be right-hand turns. The only exception is at the entrance to Edward's Ferry Park; here, make a left-hand turn onto Edward's Ferry Road. ⅄

—Jim Green

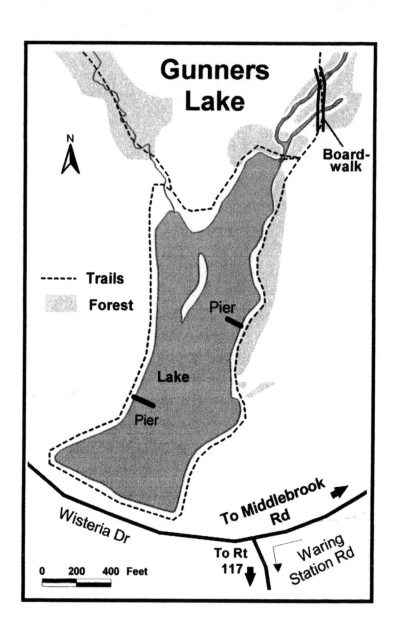

Gunners Lake

N

- - - - Trails

▨ Forest

Board-walk

Pier

Lake

Pier

Wisteria Dr

To Middlebrook Rd

To Rt 117

Waring Station Rd

0 200 400 Feet

Gunners Lake, Germantown

Surrounded by a paved walkway, Gunners Lake is a great place to visit if you have only a short time for birding or if you are bringing along small children. It is also a good place to stop and scan if you are on your way to one of the hotspots in the vicinity (Black Hill Regional Park, Seneca Creek State Park). A good mix of woodland and water birds can be found here throughout the year. In addition, several resident ducks of mixed ancestry are always conspicuous as they beg for food.

Directions: From I-270 northbound, take exit 13B, Middlebrook Road. Drive west 0.7 mile to first traffic light, Waring Station Road, and turn left. From here, it is 1.4 miles to the lake. At the first stop sign, continue straight ahead (road becomes Wisteria Drive) to lake on right.

From I-270 southbound, take exit 11, Quince Orchard Road (Route 124). At end of ramp, turn right onto Quince Orchard and drive south 0.4 mile to second traffic light, Clopper Road (Route 117). Turn right onto Clopper and proceed 2.0 miles (past entrance to Seneca Creek State Park), and turn right at traffic light onto Waring Station Road. Continue uphill 0.6 mile to stop sign and make a left onto Wisteria Drive. Lake is 0.2 mile ahead on right.

Suggested route: A walk around the lake will turn up the expected variety of backyard and woodland birds, but pleasant surprises are not uncommon. A Merlin once spent several minutes perched atop a dead tree near the far end of the lake (the part of the lake farthest away from the road), and Winter Wrens were heard and seen one spring. A Mute Swan once made an appearance.

Winter is a good time to visit, as the lake is crowded with Ring-billed Gulls and a variety of ducks, including American Wigeon, Ruddy and Ring-necked ducks, plus American Coot. One or two Canvasbacks have been present during the last few winters, as have Redheads. Belted Kingfishers and Great Blue Herons also call the lake home. In the warmer months, look for Green Herons hunting alongside their larger cousins. Be sure to check the small island in the middle of the lake; the majority of island denizens are waterfowl, but Killdeer and Spotted Sandpipers have been seen there too.

If you have time for a longer walk, there are several detours you can make as you go around the lake. If you bear right on the paved path at the far end of the lake (just as you come upon a wooden bridge), you will be led to a boardwalk. This short boardwalk traverses a small wetland, where you may find nesting Orchard Orioles, Common Yellowthroats, and flycatchers during the warmer months.

Another detour comprises a gravel path alongside a stream that runs through a narrow strip of woods. You can find this path on your left (if you walk clockwise around the lake) just as the scenery changes from houses and lawns to trees and shrubs. This path, which ends at Great Seneca Highway near Middlebrook Road, can produce warblers and other migrants in the spring, including Magnolia and Blackpoll warblers, American Redstart, Scarlet Tanager, and Wood Thrush. Y

—*Andy Rabin*

MOB '98

White-throated Sparrow

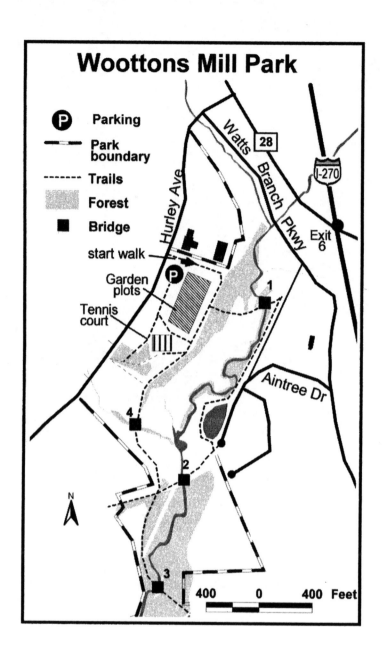

Woottons Mill Park

P Parking

— Park boundary

- - - - Trails

▨ Forest

■ Bridge

start walk

Garden plots

Tennis court

Hurley Ave

Watts Branch Pkwy

28

I-270

Exit 6

Aintree Dr

1

4

2

3

N

400 0 400 Feet

Woottons Mill Park, Rockville

N ear the intersection of I-270 and Route 28, Woottons Mill Park is good for the start of an early morning trip or a last stop on the way home. This small (76.2 acres) but varied park is surrounded by residential areas, yet still attracts large numbers of both breeding and migrant birds. More than 100 species have been counted here over a three-year period of mostly lunchtime birding on workdays. Red-shouldered Hawk, Eastern Bluebird, and both species of orioles are among the notable nesters. The best area for woodland birds is at the downstream end of the park, where Watts Branch begins its journey to the Potomac River.

Directions: From I-270 take exit 6B, Route 28 west, toward Darnestown. Take the first left onto Hurley Avenue. (There are a stoplight and a Shell station at this corner.) The park entrance, marked by a brown sign, is 0.2 mile on your left.

Suggested route: Once in the parking lot, you'll be looking downhill at a large community garden plot. The seed-bearing plants and flowers planted from spring through fall attract Chipping, Field, Savannah, Song, Swamp, and White-throated sparrows. Goldfinches, Indigo Buntings, Common Yellowthroats, and House Finches also favor the garden plots. Eastern Meadowlarks have been seen here as well. Bird all around the edges of the plots carefully—Palm and Nashville warblers have been present during migration. Scan the skies from the parking lot—a Bald Eagle was once seen flying over. Red-tailed and Red-shouldered hawks are commonly seen, as well as Broad-winged Hawks and flocks of Blue Jays during migration.

From the parking lot, follow the paved hiker/exercise trail around the edge of the garden plots to the far side. At exercise marker boards #27 and #28, walk down a steep hill through a heavily wooded area (there are enormous white oak and tulip trees on your left). The trail continues down to a footbridge, the first of four crossings over Watts Branch. The grassy fields and edges surrounding the stream are good for Baltimore Oriole, Common Yellowthroat, Eastern Towhee, Eastern Bluebird, Brown Thrasher, Gray Catbird, Eastern Kingbird, and Eastern Phoebe. Eastern Wood-Pewee and Wood Thrush are present in summer. The park's many mulberry trees sometimes attract large groups of Cedar Waxwings, while the numerous berry-producing trees and vines may lure Scarlet Tanagers and Rose-breasted Grosbeaks. Cooper's and Sharp-shinned hawks have been seen around this first crossing, and Belted Kingfishers are usually patrolling the stream.

After crossing the first bridge, continue up a slight hill. Turn right and continue on the trail, now straight and level, between thick hedgerows on the left and woods on the right. Swainson's Thrush and Veery stop here during migration, and robins, waxwings, catbirds, and towhees are usually present. Keep an eye and ear out for Downy, Hairy, Red-bellied, and Pileated woodpeckers and Yellow-shafted Flickers here and throughout the entire park. The trail continues along Aintree Drive, where the path turns to sidewalk for a short time. On the right, the newly built drainage pond is already showing cattails and other marsh vegetation. Good numbers of Spotted and Solitary sandpipers have been seen here in migration, and Mallards frequent the pond as well. An American Bittern was a surprise sighting during one spring migration.

Walk the grassy trail around the far side of the pond and bird the shrubbery. Red-shouldered Hawks are usually seen here, along with Tree, Rough-winged, and Barn swallows and Chimney Swifts in season. Brown Thrasher, Eastern Kingbird, and Eastern Phoebe are common in spring and summer. Look for woodpeckers in the dead snags along Watts Branch. An Olive-sided Flycatcher was seen here one spring.

The hiker/exercise trail resumes as you pass the pond, winding downhill under a huge sycamore tree and past a playground into a wooded area and to the second bridge crossing over Watts Branch. A White-crowned Sparrow was once seen on this path. Eastern Phoebes have nested under the bridge. Both migrating and resident birds bathe in this shallow part of the stream. Warblers seen in this area during migration include Mourning, Blue-winged, Louisiana Waterthrush, and Blackpoll. A Lincoln's Sparrow was seen here one spring. Turn left on the path after crossing the stream (keep Watts Branch to your left) and walk downhill for a few hundred yards to a third bridge over the stream. The wooded area between the bridges is the best area for warblers in migration; Magnolia, Chestnut-sided, Black-throated Green, and Black-throated Blue Warblers and

Red-shouldered Hawk   MOB '00

American Redstart have all been seen. Keep an eye out for kettles of migrating Broad-winged Hawks in fall.

Turn around at the third bridge and retrace your steps. Continue straight ahead, passing the second bridge again. A row of townhouses will be on the left, a grassy meadow on the right. Check this meadow for Indigo Bunting, Common Yellowthroat, Eastern Blue-bird, and sparrows. Also check the tall pines on your left for nuthatches. Fox Sparrows have been seen hanging around the apple tree on your left during migration. Accipiters have been seen in this area as well.

The trail continues around to the right and crosses a fourth bridge with dense thickets on either side. Orchard Orioles have nested in the shrubs on the right, and Baltimore Orioles have nested in the large weeping willow tree, also on the right. Palm Warblers have been seen in this area during migration, and Yellow Warblers nest here as well.

After crossing this last bridge, take the next left (you can also continue straight if you want to walk back around the garden). The path winds up and around through thick shrubbery, where you'll find House and Carolina wrens, Eastern Towhee, American Robin, Brown Thrasher, and Blue Jay, as well as Dark-eyed Junco and White-throated Sparrow in winter. Trumpet vine grows alongside of the path, attracting Ruby-throated Hummingbirds in late summer. The trail emerges at the top of a hill, skirts the top of the community garden, and leads back to the parking lot. Y

—*Bob Augustine/Gemma Radko*

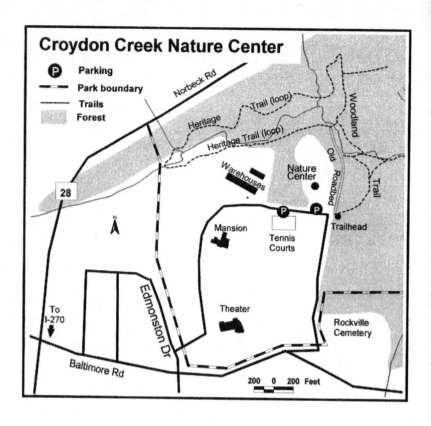

Croydon Creek Nature Center

P Parking

Park boundary

Trails

Forest

Norbeck Rd

Heritage Trail (loop)

Heritage

Heritage Trail (loop)

Woodland

Trail

28

Warehouses

Nature Center

Old Roadbed

Trailhead

Mansion

Tennis Courts

To I-270

Edmonston Dr

Theater

Rockville Cemetery

Baltimore Rd

200 0 200 Feet

Croydon Creek Nature Center, Rockville

This 120-acre tract surrounding the Rockville Civic Center was certified in 1993 as an "Urban Wildlife Sanctuary" by the U.S. Department of the Interior. Situated between Norbeck Road (Route 28) and Rockville High School, the area offers easily accessible birding for those living or working in nearby downtown Rockville.

Within the tract are a number of trails that cross ridges and follow stream valleys, leading eventually to Rock Creek Park. If you have neither the time nor the inclination to try these rigorous trails, you can bird the area suggested below and find a good variety of habitats and most of the same birds. In less than a year of birding, I have observed 125 species, including Great Horned Owl and Vesper Sparrow. Additional species will surely be added as more birders discover this area.

The newly-built Croydon Creek Nature Center is scheduled to open in the fall of 2001. Once open, it should provide a number of amenities, including new trail maps.

Directions: From I-270 north, take exit 6 onto eastbound Route 28 and follow it as it goes through downtown Rockville, across Rockville Pike (Route 355), and then over the Metro tracks to a stoplight, where Route 28 makes a 90-degree left turn and becomes First Street. Continue on First Street for 0.3 mile to the light at Baltimore Road. Turn right and drive 0.3 mile on Baltimore to Edmonston Drive. Turn left and then quickly right to enter the Civic Center grounds. Keep following the road, passing on your right the F. Scott Fitzgerald Theater and the 19th-century Glenview Mansion. Continue downhill past the tennis courts to a small parking lot on the left. If the three-to-four-car lot is full, backtrack about 100 yards and use the spaces near the tennis courts. On rare occasions, these roads may be closed due to events at the center.

The birds: Notable resident species include Pileated Woodpecker, Red-eyed and Yellow-throated vireos, Eastern Bluebird, Louisiana Waterthrush, Northern Parula, Scarlet Tanager, Indigo Bunting, and Baltimore and Orchard orioles. The site hosts Common Nighthawks in August and many Chimney Swifts in September. Fly-overs have included all expected hawk species, plus Common Loon, Killdeer, Great Egret, and Double-crested Cormorant. Fall and early winter sightings include Winter Wren, Red-breasted Nuthatch, Yellow-bellied Sapsucker, and Golden-crowned Kinglet.

MOB '95   *Dark-eyed Junco*

Suggested route: From the small parking lot there are two options: the Woodland Trail and an old roadbed for the extension of Avery Road. Both begin about 30 feet to the right of the lot, and both lead to Croydon Creek (although to different sites). The Woodland Trail, still incomplete, leads east and becomes a well-worn footpath. The roadbed, which heads north and has a wider variety of habitats, is usually more productive. Follow the roadbed downhill and then take the path that runs upstream along the creek until you emerge at the base of the vast lawn extending uphill to the mansion. Box turtles are often encountered along this trail. On the mansion grounds, carefully examine the varied edge habitat; ornamental plantings with seeds and berries attract birds, as do the pine and spruce plantings. The perimeter of the entire Civic Center grounds can be walked in about half an hour. Y

—*Bob Augustine*

Sligo Creek Park, Silver Spring

Site K

T he area of this stream valley park that will be described is the portion north of University Boulevard in Silver Spring. The north-south orientation and variety of habitats (woods, pond, stream, marsh, old field) in a relatively small area make for a nice bird walk. This park is best during spring and fall migration, when good numbers of warblers, vireos, thrushes, and flycatchers pass through. In summer there are some interesting breeding species, including Veery and (in some years) Kentucky Warbler. Winter is quiet save for the usual woodland residents, although Screech, Great Horned, and Barred owls are sometimes seen. Obviously, the best time to visit is in the early morning hours before the trails are crowded with joggers and bikers. However, one can usually find a quiet wooded path to explore at other times. Most of the trails are paved and thus wheelchair-accessible.

Directions: Heading east on I-495 (from Bethesda), take exit 31, Georgia Avenue, north toward Wheaton. Go 2.4 miles through Wheaton, crossing University Boulevard, to Arcola Avenue (library at corner). Turn right on Arcola and continue 1.4 miles. Turn right at the Lamberton Drive entrance to the Kemp Mill Shopping Center; park at the far end near Giant Food.

Heading west on I-495 (from Prince George's County), take exit 29, University Boulevard west, toward Wheaton. Go 1.6 miles past Colesville Road to the light at Arcola Avenue; turn right at Arcola. Go 0.4 mile and turn left at Lamberton Drive. Proceed as above.

Suggested route: An obvious paved path leads away from the parking lot into the park. There is an immediate T-junction: the left fork leads to two ponds with adjoining woods, the right fork to a mixed habitat of old-growth field, marsh, and upland woods. In spring, check the oaks here (as well as the ones bordering the parking lot) for warblers, including Bay-breasted. At the T, turn left (a) and continue to the two small ponds on the right, cutting around the fence and walking out on the dike. These ponds are attractive to migrants such as Solitary Sandpiper and Northern Waterthrush in spring, and often hold ducks or herons. The dike is a good platform for looking into the trees around the pond, which catch the morning sun and often hold migrants. The edge habitat here is often productive. Continuing across the dike and dam, there is a path into the woods where Veeries breed in summer.

Back on the paved path, return to the T and continue north down a slight incline. At the bottom, turn left **(b)** onto a paved trail that bisects a marshy area and then crosses Sligo Creek. This spot is especially good for warblers in migration, and Mourning Warbler has been recorded several times.

Return to the main trail and continue north. All of this area—second growth and some larger trees—can be productive. The large sycamores often support breeding Baltimore Orioles. Passing through a small woods, you come out into a larger old field (on right) with a nice marshy area on the left. Common Yellowthroats breed in the marsh most years. Take the paved trail **(c)** to the right through the open area. This old field has attracted many good birds in the past, including Blue Grosbeak, Yellow-breasted Chat, Prairie Warbler, Lincoln's Sparrow (autumn), and Olive-sided Flycatcher on the dead snags. The sunny edges should be carefully checked for feeding warblers during migration.

At the top of the field, a trail to the right enters some woods and then goes into a townhouse development. This wooded area has several boggy spots and small streams, attractive to Mourning and Golden-winged warblers in spring.

To the left, if you cross an open playing field, you will regain a (non-paved) trail **(d)** behind a row of houses. The area of high oaks and open undergrowth on the left has proved very good for migrating thrushes, especially in spring.

Where this trail meets the paved bike trail at a crossroads **(e)**, there are two options. If you continue straight ahead, you will skirt a large woodlot. The interior of this woods has had breeding Kentucky Warblers in some years, and Acadian Flycatcher, Veery, Wood Thrush, Scarlet Tanager, Ovenbird, Northern Parula, and American Redstart also breed. The edges are very good for migrants, and the open area around the school to the right is reliable for Chipping Sparrow.

Chipping Sparrow

Taking the left turn instead will put you on a the paved trail **(f)** that passes down through the woodlot. On good migration days, particularly in spring when the oaks are blooming, the woods can be alive with migrants. Listen for flocks feeding in the trees. There are many small paths leading into the woods, and these are usually worth checking. Migrants recorded here on May Counts include: Blue-winged, Golden-winged, Canada, Nashville, Worm-eating, Black-throated Blue, Black-throated Green, Blackpoll, Black-and-white, Blackburnian and Cape May warblers, Black-billed Cuckoo, Yellow-throated Vireo, and Gray-cheeked Thrush.

This trail eventually loops around and meets intersection **(c)**. From there you can retrace your steps to the parking lot.

—Gail Mackiernan

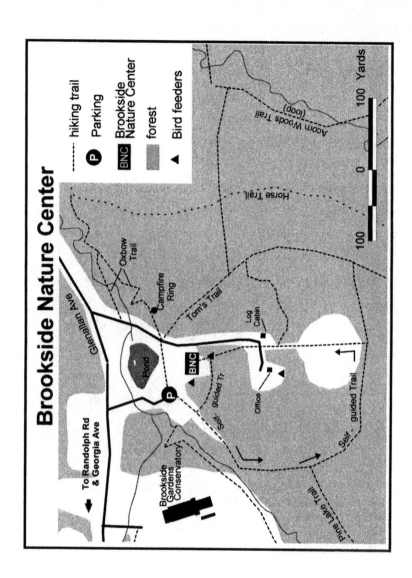

Brookside Nature Center

hiking trail
P Parking
BNC Brookside Nature Center
forest
▲ Bird feeders

100 Yards

Acorn Woods Trail (loop)

Horse Trail

Oxbow Trail

Glenallan Ave

Campfire Ring

Tom's Trail

Log Cabin

Pond

BNC

P

Office

Self- guided Tr

Self- guided Trail

To Randolph Rd & Georgia Ave

Brookside Gardens Conservatory

Pine Lake Trail

Brookside Nature Center, Wheaton

Wheaton Regional Park, bounded by Georgia Avenue on the west, Glenallan Avenue on the north, Kemp Mill Road on the east, and Arcola Avenue on the south, is a largely forested area of some 536 acres. The park complex includes a recreation area (Shorefield area) and botanical gardens (Brookside Gardens) both of which have good birding possibilities. However, for those with a limited amount of time, the most productive birding areas are found on the trails surrounding the Brookside Nature Center.

Directions: From I-495 take exit 31, Georgia Avenue, and drive north for 3.1 miles. At the intersection of Georgia Avenue and Randolph Road, proceed east on Randolph Road. Turn right at the traffic signal onto Glenallan Avenue. After .04 mile you will reach a stop sign (at the entrance to Brookside Gardens Visitor Center). Continue east on Glenallan for .02 mile (past a second entrance to the gardens) and turn into the Nature Center on your right.

The Nature Center is open Tuesday–Sunday, closed Mondays and holidays. Call 301–946–9071 for hours of operation. At the center (handicapped accessible), you can pick up a trail map and a checklist of some 140 species that have been seen here, including 58 known breeders. The center offers a variety of programs for all ages, including bird walks. Nighttime "owl prowls," led by park naturalists, have yielded Screech, Barred, and Great Horned owls.

Suggested routes: Check the trees surrounding the parking lot for warblers and tanagers in migration. A paved trail leads from the corner of the parking lot closest to the building past a small pond on your left. Check for Wood Duck, Mallard, and Canada Goose; sometimes a Belted Kingfisher will buzz by. This is also a good place to look for Solitary and Spotted sandpipers in spring. Continue on the paved trail and cross the service road. Along the way you will pass a hummingbird garden and nectar feeders, always worth checking in summer and early fall.

From this point, there are two marked trail options. To the left, the Oxbow Trail makes a short loop through a swampy area and can be good for Wood and Swainson's thrushes. Another trail good for woodland birds is the circular Acorn Woods Trail, just right for an hour's walk (about 1.25 miles round trip). To reach Acorn Woods Trail, follow Tom's Trail uphill and turn left at the first trail junction. After about 300 yards, Tom's Trail dead-ends at the Acorn Woods Trail. Going in either direction will bring you back to this point. In winter, either trail can yield most of the local woodpeckers, White-breasted Nuthatch, Brown Creeper, and Winter Wren.

MOB '99

Sharp-shinned Hawk (left) and Cooper's Hawk

The self-guided nature trail, a short loop behind the Nature Center, is especially fruitful during spring and fall migration. Starting at the center's back door, go up the steps, turn right, and follow the trail signs. The path travels through woods and a small meadow. The meadow edges can be good for warblers such as Northern Parula, Magnolia,and Black-and-white. In fall, check the meadow for Field and Swamp sparrows and the occasional Lincoln's (seen several times in October). In appropriate seasons and habitats, look for Red-eyed and White-eyed vireos, Golden-crowned and Ruby-crowned kinglets, Cedar Waxwing, Bluebird, and White-throated and Song sparrows. Be sure to glance overhead for the occasional Red-tailed, Red-shouldered or Cooper's hawk.

If you have the time, plan to visit nearby Brookside Gardens. The two indoor conservatories, housing mainly tropical plants, hold attractive seasonal displays. Begin your walk on the paved path that winds through the adjacent 50-acre horticultural display gardens. The best birding areas are the wooded sections. In spring, the larger trees near the building can hold warblers, vireos, and tanagers. As you move along, continue to check the wood edges, where you might spot Common Yellowthroat, American Redstart, or Black-throated Blue Warbler. In winter, follow the signs leading to Pine Lake, at most a ten-minute walk from the building. The five-acre lake, well stocked with fish, can yield an assortment of winter water-fowl, including Mallard, American Black Duck, Pied-billed Grebe, and an occasional Northern Pintail or Hooded Merganser. ⅄

—*Barbara Holloman*

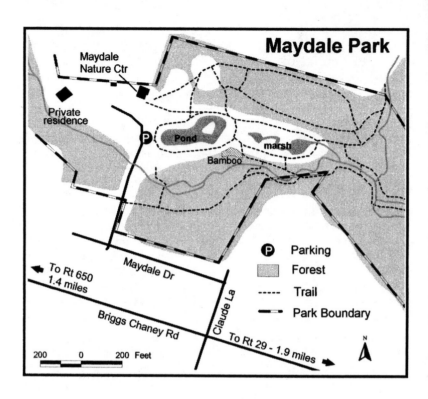

Maydale Park

Maydale
Nature Ctr

Private
residence

Pond

marsh

Bamboo

To Rt 650
1.4 miles

Maydale Dr

Briggs Chaney Rd

Claude La

To Rt 29 - 1.9 miles

P Parking

Forest

----- Trail

Park Boundary

200   0   200 Feet

N

Maydale Park, Cloverly

M aydale Park packs many varied habitats into a small oasis in the middle of suburbia. The area was once owned by the Izaak Walton League and used as a meeting place and shooting range. Surrounding development eventually limited these uses and the land was donated to the county park system. Conservation work done by the League created a pond, freshwater marsh, white pine plantation, and a mix of field, forest, and hedgerows that continues to provide food and shelter for a variety of wildlife species.

Directions: From I-495, take exit 28A, New Hampshire Avenue (Route 650), north. After crossing Route 29, continue about 4 miles and turn right onto Good Hope Road. After approximately 1.3 miles, turn right onto Briggs Chaney Road. Go 0.5 mile and turn left onto Claude Lane; continue for one block and turn left onto Maydale Drive. After one block, turn right into the park driveway, proceed to the bottom of the hill, and park in the lot.

The area: Since the Department of Education uses the park as an outdoor classroom for field trips, it is best to avoid the area between 10 a.m. and 3 p.m. on school days. Maydale Nature Center, the building at the top of the hill, is generally not open to the public. A portable toilet in the parking lot is the only facility available to the public.

Suggested route: A maze of trails (see map) offers many possible routes that can easily be covered in an hour or two. I usually start by scanning the area around the pond, which is off to the right as you enter the parking lot. Go through the split-rail fence, bear right through the pines, and begin to circle the pond counter-clockwise. Great Blue and Green herons, Belted Kingfisher, Mallard, Canada Goose, and Eastern Phoebe are often present, as well as Spotted and Solitary sandpipers during migration. Muskrat—and in recent years a beaver—are residents that are most likely to be seen at dusk or very early in the morning. Red-shouldered Hawks nest in the woods to your right and are often heard and seen soaring overhead.

After scanning the pond, walk back to the pines and go left on a trail that leads into the woods. On a sunny morning this wood edge can be an active spot. Depending on the season, the ever-present Carolina Chickadees, Tufted Titmice, Carolina Wrens, and Northern Cardinals may be joined by Ruby-crowned and Golden-crowned kinglets, Blue-gray Gnatcatchers, Red-eyed and Yellow-throated vireos, and any number of migrants. Continue into the woods and cross the bridge. This little stream is part of Paint Branch, one of the cleanest and healthiest stream systems in the county. Follow the trail to the top of a little hill and turn left onto a trail that is good for woodland species. Breeding birds that you may see here include all of our nesting woodpeckers, Eastern Wood-Pewee, Great Crested and Acadian flycatchers, and Ovenbird.

From this trail, take one of several left turns to re-cross the stream and circle the small marsh area adjacent to the pond. A number of trails lead uphill to younger woods and hedgerows that are good for Eastern Towhee, sparrows, and other edge species. A patch of white pines above the marsh has produced a Barred Owl on several occasions. Following the map, work your way back toward the nature center, which usually has stocked bird feeders. ⅄

—*Rob Gibbs*

Eastern Wood-Pewee   MOB

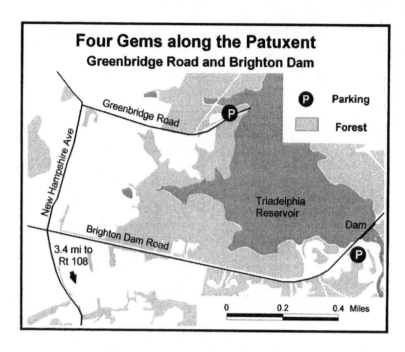

Four Gems along the Patuxent
Greenbridge Road and Brighton Dam

Greenbridge Road

P Parking

Forest

New Hampshire Ave

Triadelphia Reservoir

Dam

Brighton Dam Road

3.4 mi to Rt 108

0   0.2   0.4 Miles

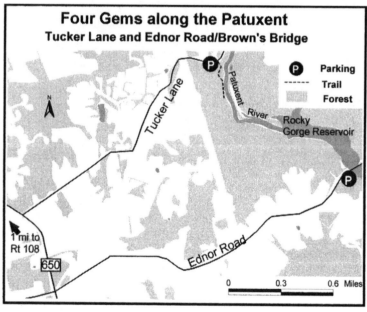

Four Gems along the Patuxent
Tucker Lane and Ednor Road/Brown's Bridge

Tucker Lane

Patuxent River

P Parking

------ Trail

Forest

Rocky Gorge Reservoir

N

1 mi to Rt 108

650

Ednor Road

0   0.3   0.6 Miles

Four Gems along the Patuxent

Site N

T he four sites described here are located along the Patuxent River off New Hampshire Avenue (Route 650), north of Silver Spring. The first two, Greenbridge Road and Brighton Dam, are north of Route 108 and offer the birder different views of Triadelphia Reservoir; they are best visited for waterfowl from late fall to early spring. The other two sites, Tucker Lane and Ednor Road, are south of Route 108 and are good for neotropical migrants and shorebirds during spring, summer, and early fall. All four are watershed properties maintained by the WSSC; please respect all "No Trespassing" signs.

The starting point for all four sites is the intersection of Route 108 and New Hampshire Avenue (Route 650) in Ashton. From I-495, take exit 28, New Hampshire Avenue (Route 650), and head north for approximately 11 miles.

Greenbridge Road and Brighton Dam

Directions: To reach Greenbridge Road from the above intersection, head north on Route 650 for 3.8 miles to Greenbridge Road and turn right. In 0.5 mile, you will reach a metal gate. (Note: The gate is closed during the no-fishing season, December 16-February 28, and between dusk and dawn at all times.) Proceed another 0.1 mile to the parking lot.

Suggested route: Begin by checking the trees surrounding the lot for woodpeckers and the usual winter foraging flocks. In late March and early April, examine the pine trees on your right, as you face the water, for Pine Warblers.

Then take your scope down to the water's edge, setting it up well away from the boat ramp. Late fall to early winter and late winter to early spring are the best times for finding birds on the water. In April and early May, look for migrating Common Loons in breeding plumage; early in the morning you may hear their eerie yodeling. This area is good for viewing Common Mergansers—regular winter visitors found in good numbers—and Red-breasted Mergansers, found in smaller numbers. Occasionally you may find Bufflehead, Long-tailed Duck, Red-throated Loon, and Eurasian Wigeon.

For another perspective on the reservoir, return to the parking lot. At the top corner of the lot near the two portable toilets is an overflow parking lot. Walk through this lot, keeping to the right, to a fire road and follow it to the end. In addition to checking here for waterfowl, look along the left side of the reservoir in line with the radio tower for an active Bald Eagle nest in a large deciduous tree. (Note that this nest is in Howard County; for a Montgomery County nest, see "Bald Eagle Watch, Great Falls.") Two years ago, an adult Bald Eagle flew over the reservoir, followed by a Peregrine Falcon. Along the fire road, look for vireos, warblers, and thrushes in migration and woodpeckers, Eastern Bluebirds, and the occasional owl in winter.

To reach Brighton Dam Road, return to New Hampshire Avenue, turn left, and go about 0.4 mile south to Brighton Dam Road. Turn left and go 1.0 mile to the lot at the Brighton Dam Information Center. With newly resurfaced roads and sidewalks, this is a perfect place to set up a scope and look for Ospreys, eagles, Caspian Terns, and Common Loons.

This is also one of the few reliable places in the county to find Cliff Swallows, which usually appear by the third week in April. They nest under the dam and can be seen flying in and out; at times they fly along the concrete wall, swooping up insects above the grass. Below the dam, check the picnic grounds for waders, kingfishers, other swallows, and Eastern Phoebe. This is also a good place for butterflies in summer.

Hooded Warbler

Tucker Lane

Directions: To reach Tucker Lane from the junction of Route 108 and Route 650, head south (right) on Route 650 for 0.95 mile to Tucker Lane and turn left, going 1.5 miles to a gravel shoulder on the right. Park and look for the WSSC sign marked Tucker Lane. Take the small (occasionally overgrown) trail that begins here.

Suggested route: After an incline, the trail goes down to a small ravine (a good place for Hooded Warbler), and back up the other side, then winds down the embankment. Be alert for slippery rocks and poison ivy! From the river's edge, head downriver, crossing a small creek (look for Louisiana Waterthrush), and continue through the woods. The trail will lead to a rocky outcrop on the left that juts out over the Patuxent. This is a beautiful spot to look up and down the river for migrants. Check also the open woods between the creek and the outcropping for migrants and local breeders such as Acadian Flycatcher, Yellow-throated and Blue-headed vireos, Blue-gray Gnatcatcher, and Northern Parula. The deeper woods on the right beyond the outcropping are good for thrushes and Ovenbird.

Return to your starting point and head upriver. Here the habitat changes to smaller, second-growth trees with a heavy understory of shrubs and vines. Following the overgrown trail can be difficult, but with persistence you may be rewarded with Red-eyed and White-eyed vireos and an occasional Philadelphia Vireo in season, as well as warblers. The trail winds close to the river in some places, affording nice views of a series of small rapids upriver. Look here for Spotted Sandpipers and herons and a possible Osprey. At a point just before the rapids, a creek flows into the Patuxent from the left. A small trail parallels this creek and heads back to Tucker Lane, a distance of perhaps 50 yards. You can follow it back to the road or, if you are feeling adventurous, continue exploring upstream for a while.

Once back on Tucker Lane, it pays to walk a quarter mile above and below where you parked, checking the woods on both sides of the road. Just standing still, you might spot warblers high in the trees. Also possible here, in addition to woodpeckers, tanagers, fly-over hawks, and herons, are Hooded and Kentucky warblers, Yellow-throated Vireo, and Yellow-breasted Chat.

Ednor Road at Brown's Bridge

Directions: Beginning again at the intersection of Route 650 and Route 108, go 1.4 miles south on New Hampshire Avenue. Turn left and head east on Ednor Road for 1.9 miles to a parking/boat ramp sign on the right. Best from late August through early October, this area can be productive as early as mid-July for shorebirds, raptors, and waders.

Suggested route: Walk to the end of the boat ramp. In late summer the low water levels can create mudflats for shorebirds, seen mostly below the bridge. Birding from the bridge itself is unsafe and unproductive because of the heavy traffic. From mid-July through August, almost any shorebird on the county list could be expected here, but good finds include Solitary Sandpiper, both yellowlegs, Semipalmated, Western, Least, and Pectoral sandpipers, Killdeer, Semipalmated Plover, and (once) a Stilt Sandpiper. Look overhead for raptors; Northern Harrier, Osprey, Bald Eagle, Cooper's and Sharp-shinned hawks are possible. Check also for long-legged waders, including both Black-crowned and Yellow-crowned night-herons. A small foot trail next to the boat ramp, going to the right as you face the river, leads off through woods where Yellow-billed Cuckoos are likely; Olive-sided Flycatcher was reported here one fall. Ỵ

—Rick Sussman

Semipalmated (left) and White-rumped sandpipers   MOB '99

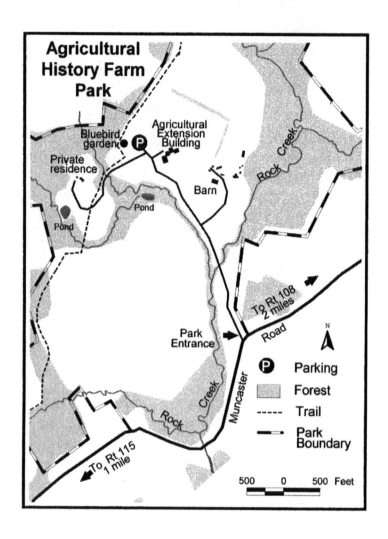

Agricultural History Farm Park

Bluebird garden
Agricultural Extension Building
Private residence
Pond
Pond
Barn
Rock Creek
Park Entrance
To Rt 108 2 miles
Road
Muncaster
Rock Creek
To Rt 115 1 mile
N

P Parking
Forest
Trail
Park Boundary

500   0   500 Feet

Agricultural History Farm Park, Derwood

T he Agricultural History Farm Park was established to promote an appreciation for Montgomery County's farming heritage; on weekends throughout the year, the staff conducts farm-related festivals and activities. The large, open grass fields, hedgerows, wood edges, and small streams in the park provide good birding opportunities, especially during spring migration and the early nesting season, from late April until mid-June. Birds of interest (aside from the common edge species) include American Kestrel, Red-tailed Hawk, Eastern Bluebird, Tree and Barn swallows, Willow Flycatcher, Yellow Warbler, Yellow-breasted Chat, Grasshopper Sparrow, Eastern Meadowlark, and Baltimore Oriole.

Directions: From I-270, take exit 8, Shady Grove Road, and drive east 3.5 miles to Muncaster Mill Road (Route 115). Turn right on Muncaster Mill, drive 0.25 mile to Muncaster Road, and turn left. Go 1.25 miles and turn left onto park entrance road. Continue straight ahead approximately 0.5 mile, past the Cooperative Extension Building on the right, to where the road ends in a parking lot. The park is open most days from sunrise to sunset but is occasionally closed for special events. The Cooperative Extension Building, open most weekdays from 9 a.m. to 5 p.m., has restrooms and a water fountain.

Suggested route: The following route takes about an hour and gives a taste of the mostly open habitat in this park. If you like what you see and have the time, you could spend several hours on the mowed trails maintained around most of the wood and field borders.

Before you leave the parking lot, note the adjacent garden area designed to provide habitat for Bluebirds. (The many nest boxes throughout the park are well used by Bluebirds and Tree Swallows.)

From the parking lot, bird your way back down the road to the park entrance, about half a mile. The hedgerow and small stream that parallel the road on the right offer habitat for Willow Flycatcher, White-eyed Vireo, Yellow Warbler, and other typical edge species. About halfway down the drive on the right, there is a ford for farm equipment to enter the fields. This is a popular place for birds to drink and bathe. It can also be a fantastic spot to see butterflies such as clouded and orange sulfurs, cabbage whites, tiger swallowtails, and skippers "puddling" (gathering in numbers to ingest nutrients from moist soil). About a hundred yards farther down the drive, you will cross a bridge over Rock Creek. Check the area around the bridge for Baltimore and, occasionally, Orchard orioles. Both species may also show up in the large trees near the park entrance.

Upon reaching the end of the entrance road, backtrack and take the gravel road to the right, leading up toward the large red barn. Where the gravel road passes between two outbuildings, there is an American Kestrel box on a telephone pole to the left that is active in most years. Past the box, on the right, are several demonstration garden areas maintained by the Cooperative Extension Service's Master Gardeners. The large grass fields beyond the gardens are good for Grasshopper Sparrow and an occasional Eastern Meadowlark. If you don't see them here, you can work your way out into the fields, but watch for ticks. The easiest way, however, is to return to the parking lot and then walk the wood edge. Mowed trails are usually maintained along the wood edge, but this varies through the summer.

If you have extra time, walk the gravel drive to the right as you leave the parking lot. It leads to an area of mixed woods and a field with a small pond, and ultimately to a park house leased as a private residence. Walk only as far as the pond, respecting the privacy of the residents. Retrace your steps to the parking lot. ⅄

—*Rob Gibbs*

Grasshopper Sparrow

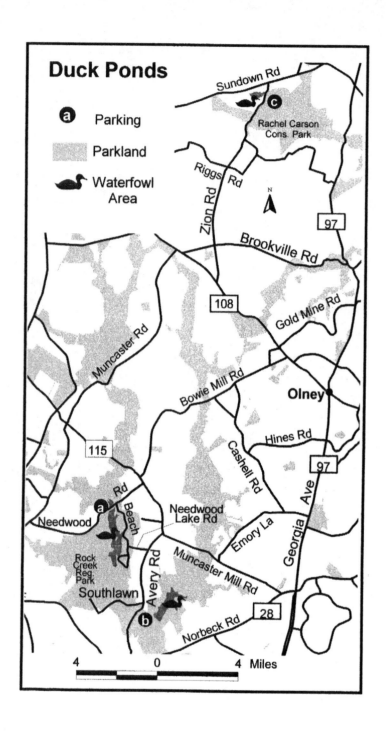

Duck Ponds

a Parking

Parkland

Waterfowl Area

Sundown Rd

c Rachel Carson Cons. Park

Riggs Rd

Zion Rd

N

97

Brookville Rd

108

Gold Mine Rd

Muncaster Rd

Bowie Mill Rd

Olney

Hines Rd

115

Cashell Rd

97

Georgia Ave

Rd

Beach

a Needwood

Needwood Lake Rd

Emory La

Rock Creek Reg. Park

Muncaster Mill Rd

Avery Rd

Southlawn

b

Norbeck Rd

28

4   0   4 Miles

Duck Ponds, Eastern Montgomery County

Site P

For those who live in the eastern part of the county and do not want to travel to Black Hill Regional Park or the C&O Canal to look for winter waterfowl, there are three sites in the eastern portion of the county where these birds tend to congregate. The first two stops, Lake Needwood and Lake Bernard Frank, are man-made lakes in parks maintained by the M-NCPPC. The last stop is near a pond on private property, without an official name, but referred to by birders as "Zion Road Pond."

Lake Needwood

Directions: From I-495, take exit 31A, Georgia Avenue (Route 97), and drive north approximately 10 miles. Turn left onto Norbeck Road (Route 28), go 0.2 mile, and turn right onto Muncaster Mill Road (Route 115). Continue for 2.9 miles and turn left at traffic light at Needwood Road. In 0.6 mile you will reach a bridge that crosses the end of Lake Needwood. Pull over to wide shoulder on right and park near bridge.

From I-270, take exit 8, Shady Grove Road, and follow signs to an immediate right onto Redland Boulevard. From the first traffic light (Piccard Drive), proceed 1.8 miles, crossing Route 355, and turn right at traffic light at Needwood Road. Continue 1.5 miles to bridge. Cross bridge and park as described above.

Suggested route: The morning light here is not too good, but it pays to scan both sides of the bridge for waterfowl such as Ruddy and Ring-necked ducks, shorebirds, long-legged waders, and raptors. In winter, walk back along the guard rail to the metal gate on your left and follow the grassy area to the right of the lake and bridge; this is excellent habitat for Fox Sparrow (fall and spring), Chipping and Field sparrows, Dark-eyed Junco, and Eastern Towhee. In late winter and early spring this is a good place to search for Wood Duck, Blue-winged Teal, Northern Shoveler, and Hooded Merganser. In this season it is also worth checking the pine woods on the other side of the bridge for nesting or roosting owls.

For another view of the main body of the lake, with better lighting, return to your car and make a U-turn, taking the first right onto Beach Drive (the road sign may be missing; look for a brown M-NCPPC sign) into the park. In 0.5 mile you will see the lake on your right; park in the spaces along the roadway. Take your scope and walk across a long footbridge to the field on your right. This is good sparrow habitat: White-throated, Song, and Field sparrows are likely; American Tree Sparrow is possible. This walk will take you to a point of land from which you can scope a good portion of the lake. There are usually large numbers of Canada Geese, Mallards, Ring-necked Ducks, Buffleheads, and Ruddy Ducks, along with smaller numbers of American Black Ducks, American Wigeon, and Hooded Mergansers. Pied-billed Grebes, Great Blue Herons, American Coots, and Belted Kingfishers are likely too.

Lake Frank

From Lake Needwood it is a short drive to Lake Frank. Although smaller than Needwood, Lake Frank can be just as productive.

Directions: Take Beach Drive for 0.25 mile to the T-intersection with Needwood Lake Road and turn left. Continue on Needwood Lake Road to the end and turn right onto Avery Road. Drive 0.8 mile to the intersection with Southlawn Lane and continue 0.1 mile to a brown sign on your left indicating parking for Lake Frank. Park at the far end of the lot.

Suggested route: Take your scope and follow the marked trail downhill to the dam at the end of the lake. Frequently the birds are some distance away, so a powerful scope is helpful. In winter, this spot is usually good only for waterfowl. From early October on, look for Green-winged Teal, American Wigeon, American Coot, and Ruddy and Ring-necked ducks. At times you may find Common Merganser or Pied-billed Grebe. If you return in spring, you can begin a hike from here around the lake (via the Lakeshore Trail); the woods surrounding the lake can be alive with migrants such as vireos, thrushes, warblers, tanagers, and orioles.

Ring-necked Ducks

Zion Road Pond

By now it should be mid-morning and a good time to visit the Zion Road pond in Sunshine, west of Olney.

Directions: Take Avery Road back 1.3 miles to the intersection with Muncaster Mill Road and turn left at the light. In 1.0 mile, turn right at Bowie Mill Road. Continue past two stop signs to Route 108 and turn left. After 1.6 miles, turn right onto Zion Road and proceed 0.5 mile to a stop sign. Go straight and continue for 2.6 miles, crossing a small one-lane bridge over a creek, a tributary of the Hawlings River. The woods on your right are part of the Rachel Carson Conservation Park (see site description). Continue until you see a large pond on the left. Because there are no shoulders on this narrow road, parking can be difficult. You can either pull as far as possible to the right, next to the woods, or turn around and park on the grassy strip between the fence and the road. If the grass is wet or muddy, be sure to keep at least two wheels on dry pavement. Please respect this privately owned land and stay outside the fence.

Features: Mainly a deep-water pond except at the shallower eastern end, Zion Road pond attracts mostly diving ducks, although anything can show up. When Lakes Needwood and Frank are devoid of birds, this spot may often hold them. And because local rarities sometimes show up here, it can pay to visit the pond several times in a single morning anytime between October and April. Throughout the season you can expect to find Canada Goose, American Black Duck, Mallard, American Wigeon, Ring-necked Duck, Bufflehead, Hooded Merganser, and Ruddy Duck. Less often, Tundra Swan, Snow Goose, Wood Duck, Greater and Lesser scaup, Canvasback, Redhead, and Long-tailed Duck may also be present. The grassy area adjacent to the pond should be checked for Eastern Phoebes and Eastern Bluebirds, which frequently perch in small trees in the yard of the large house on the left. Check overhead for vultures and raptors. Υ

—*Rick Sussman*

The Birding Year in Montgomery County

JANUARY

- Check reservoirs for Common Loon as well as the occasional Red-throated Loon. Also search for grebes: both Pied-billed and Horned grebes are likely, and in severe winters, Red-necked Grebe is possible.

- Great Blue Herons overwinter. Check pond edges for open water.

- Scan large bodies of water for wintering waterfowl, especially Tundra Swan, Canvasback, Redhead, Ring-necked Duck, and Common Goldeneye. Black Hill Regional Park and Zion Road pond can be productive.

- Study flocks of Canada Geese for the occasional Snow Goose (either color morph is possible) and, more rarely, Greater White-fronted Goose.

- A prolonged freeze can produce an amazing variety of water-fowl on any open spots in the ice. A scope may be necessary for best viewing. Check especially Black Hill.

- Hawks may be more in evidence, perched on bare branches over open fields, Red-tailed high, and Red-shouldered usually lower. Sharp-shinned and Cooper's hawks are regular in small numbers. Look for American Kestrels on utility wires in the countryside. At least one (perhaps as many as three) Merlin wintered in Silver Spring in the late 1990s; check dead snags for the falcon's upright posture, especially towards dusk or on rainy or overcast days. Rough-legged Hawks occasionally show up in severe winters.

- Check shallow pond edges and wet swales for Killdeer and the occasional Common Snipe.

- Gulls are easiest to find in January, February, and early March. Besides Ring-billed and Herring, look along the Potomac for Great Black-backed, more rarely Lesser Black-backed, and sometimes Bonaparte's.

- January is a good time to search for owls. Great Horned Owls are already courting and begin nesting as early as mid-month; study large stick nests in deciduous woods for "horns" sticking up above the rim. Barred Owls, which begin courting late in the month, can be very vocal at dawn and dusk, especially near wet woods. Eastern Screech-Owls sometimes respond to tapes. Explore pine groves and honeysuckle tangles on wooded lots for Northern Saw-whet Owls, usually present but infrequently seen or heard. Also check pine/conifer thickets for Long-eared Owls, not found every year; search the ground for pellets and whitewash.

- A winter walk through the woods and fields should produce an array of woodpeckers, including many Downy, fewer Hairy, and good numbers of Red-bellied, Northern Flicker, and Pileated (especially along the C&O Canal). Yellow-bellied Sapsuckers are regular winter visitors. Red-headed Woodpeckers are increasingly hard to find.

- In mild winters, look for Eastern Phoebes in warm spots near open water.

- Mixed feeding flocks can include Carolina Chickadee, Tufted Titmouse, White-breasted Nuthatch, Brown Creeper, Carolina Wren, Golden-crowned and Ruby-crowned kinglets, and perhaps Yellow-rumped Warbler.

- Winter Wrens turn up in wet, overgrown areas and tangles near streams. The canal is a good spot to look for them.

- Winter sparrow regulars are Field, Song, and White-throated, along with Dark-eyed Junco and Eastern Towhee. Less common are American Tree, Chipping, Fox, Swamp, and White-crowned sparrows. Layhill Park can be productive, especially the south fields.

- Search for wintertime irruptive finches along and near swales with alders, whose catkins produce seed relished by Purple Finches, Common—and more rarely, Hoary—redpolls, American Goldfinches, and American Tree Sparrows. Small flocks of crossbills can sometimes be spotted as they zip from one stand of pines to another. Pine Siskins and Evening Grosbeaks sometimes join other finches at feeders.

FEBRUARY

- February can be a difficult month for birds and birding, as the county sometimes records its coldest temperatures and food can be scarce. Still, survey open bodies of water for Tundra Swan (especially at Black Hill), Snow Goose, and ducks such as Green-winged Teal, Gadwall, American Wigeon, Canvasback, Red-head, and Common Goldeneye. Common and Red-breasted mergansers frequent Triadelphia Reservoir and the Potomac River.

- By month's end, American Woodcock can be heard "peenting" in weedy fields with scattered small trees and shrubs, preferably near a woodlot. Their display flights are a sure sign that spring is on its way.

- Before the month is out, Eastern Screech-Owls will begin courting; listen for their quavering tremolo song early in the morning and again at dusk. Barred Owls become more vocal this month.

- Winter-hardy songbirds—Eastern Bluebirds, Hermit Thrushes, and American Robins—spend the month foraging for whatever fruit they can find. Keep an eye out for both kinglet species, as well as Brown Creeper, Yellow-rumped Warbler, and American Tree Sparrow.

- Common Grackles arrive by mid-month, flocks of males first.

MARCH

- March birding is a mixed bag; many winter residents are more noticeable, and some early spring migrants begin filtering in. Investigate local ponds and reservoirs often, especially after storms or weather fronts, as the species can change daily.

- Both Pied-billed and Horned grebes appear in small numbers as they make their way north. Red-necked Grebes can show up if lakes farther north are frozen.

- Look for Wood Duck, both teal species, and Hooded Merganser, as well as locally uncommon Northern Pintail and Northern Shoveler. The former is best found at Hughes Hollow, while the latter can be sought at Seneca Creek State Park or the north end of Lake Needwood.

- Northern Harriers and Sharp-shinned and Cooper's hawks are more in evidence, along with Red-shouldered Hawks, Red-tailed Hawks, and American Kestrels.

- American Coots start appearing in small numbers (though a few may have wintered over).

- Killdeer are coming back; listen for their "kidee" calls overhead at night.

- Common Snipe begin passing through by mid-month. Explore the edges of shallow ponds and wet grassy fields. Sycamore Landing Road is often rewarding.

- Mid-March to late April is the best time to observe the display flights of American Woodcock. Check weedy fields, especially near Hughes Hollow and Little Bennett Regional Park.

- Continue to seek out Yellow-bellied Sapsucker, Red-headed Woodpecker (increasingly rare), and Northern Flicker. Try Black Hill for a seven-woodpecker day!

- Eastern Phoebe numbers are on the rise; some may have wintered locally.

- Swallows begin to arrive. Tree Swallows are usually the first, followed by Northern Rough-winged and a few Purple Martins. Check the impoundments at Hughes Hollow.

- Winter Wrens are still around; take note of rooty tangles in streamside woods.

- Eastern Bluebirds are staking out territories and claiming nest sites. Make sure nest boxes are cleaned out. American Robins return to suburban lawns.

- Mid-month sees American Pipits coming through. They can appear almost anywhere, but check short grassy fields and perhaps golf courses.

- Along with Yellow-rumped Warblers, Pine Warblers begin to appear and sing; listen for their musical trill in pine woods, though they can show up in deciduous woods as well.

- Look for lingering American Tree, Savannah, and White-crowned sparrows. The last two prefer shrubby fields, or open fields with hedgerow borders. Fox and Swamp sparrows arrive toward month's end.

- Red-winged Blackbirds join the throng, males first, early in the month.

APRIL

- The busy season gets under way, as migrants flood in almost continuously. Many of the earliest arrivals are half-hardy birds that spend winter months in the warmer southeastern states. These include Double-crested Cormorant, Green Heron, Osprey, Tree Swallow, Ruby-crowned Kinglet, Blue-gray Gnatcatcher, Blue-headed Vireo, and warblers—Northern Parula, Yellow-throated, Pine, Palm, and Prairie—as well as Eastern Towhee.

- From mid-April through mid-May, Common Loons stop by on large reservoirs, where they can be heard "yodeling" in the early morning. Most wear alternate plumage, though some may retain traces of basic plumage.

- American Bitterns pass through late in the month. Some remain for a few days, even a week or more, in areas with heavy cattail growth. Least Bitterns also return. Check Hughes Hollow and the wet fields along Sycamore Landing Road.

- Green Herons begin trickling in; by month's end, nearly every body of water seems to hold at least one or two. Yellow-crowned Night-Herons also stage a comeback, though they appear only sporadically in the county. Visit Sycamore Landing Road or Sligo Creek Parkway west of Piney Branch Road (where they have nested in recent years).

- Waterfowl numbers drop off, but ponds and lakes may still host Blue-winged Teal, Long-tailed Duck, Ruddy Duck, and other lingerers. Female Common and Red-breasted mergansers may remain on reservoirs long after the males have left.

- Expect to see increasing numbers of Osprey, Bald Eagle, Northern Harrier, Sharp-shinned Hawk, and American Kestrel. The occasional Peregrine Falcon can show up almost anywhere. Around mid-month, Broad-winged Hawks begin to move through; flocks are usually smaller than in autumn, with any-where from one to thirty or more birds. Both Black and Turkey vultures are more numerous, too.

- Chances of hearing and even seeing Wild Turkey and Ring-necked Pheasant increase. Northern Bobwhite often call in the morning, sometimes until midday. Triadelphia Lake Road is a good place to look for all three species. Also try Hughes Hollow, Sycamore Landing Road, and Little Bennett.

- American Coot numbers are building.

- Check local ponds for shorebirds, which come through in small numbers into early May. You can expect Greater and Lesser yellowlegs and Solitary and Pectoral sandpipers. Killdeer are on the increase, while some Common Snipe may linger.

- Later in the month, while scanning ponds for waterfowl, you will likely encounter Caspian Terns and Bonaparte's Gulls as well as swallows, including Northern Rough-winged, Barn, Cliff, and finally Bank. Ponds surrounded by fields are good for all except Cliff, which can be found reliably at Brighton Dam.

- Hummingbird feeders should be cleaned and put out by mid-month. Male Ruby-throated Hummingbirds arrive first, followed a week or two later by the females. Early-blooming azaleas and bleeding heart will attract them to your yard.

- Eastern Phoebe numbers swell and Eastern Kingbirds and Acadian Flycatchers begin to arrive. Try Hughes Hollow for an early Willow Flycatcher.

- Other common birds returning this month: White-eyed and Red-eyed vireos, House Wren, Brown Thrasher, Gray Catbird, and a host of warbler species, including Yellow, Black-throated Blue, Black-throated Green, Yellow-throated, Black-and-white, American Redstart, Ovenbird, Louisiana Waterthrush, Common Yellowthroat, and Hooded. Orchard Orioles arrive by the third week, followed by Baltimore Orioles and Scarlet Tanagers.

- Blue Jays and American Crows, and to a lesser extent Fish Crows, are more evident, as are Belted Kingfisher, Northern Flicker, American Robin, Cedar Waxwing, Red-winged Blackbird, and Common Grackle.

- Small numbers of Red-breasted Nuthatches migrate through early to mid-month. Search especially stands of pines and other conifers. Check Little Bennett and Seneca Creek parks.

- Overgrown fields and wet fields with small shrubs can produce a variety of sparrows: Chipping, Field, Savannah, Swamp, and

White-crowned, along with the more common Song and White-throated. By the end of the month, most Dark-eyed Juncos will be gone. Triadelphia Lake Road is a good place to look, as are Hughes Hollow, Layhill Park, and around the first impound-ment at Pennyfield Lock on the canal.

• By month's end, Bobolinks begin filtering in, males first. Numbers will peak around Mother's Day. Check large expanses of grassy (uncut) fields. Flocks of as many as 60 or more have been seen (and heard!) regularly along Triadelphia Lake Road.

MAY

• The busy season is now in full swing, as birds head north to nesting grounds, with many species settling here in the county to breed.

• Common Loons frequently linger at Black Hill Regional Park and Triadelphia Reservoir until about mid-month.They are usu-ally an early-morning migrant, and can sometimes be heard calling in flight.

• Double-crested Cormorants move up the Potomac and Patuxent river valleys and begin to disperse onto larger bodies of water.

• Green Herons can be seen on almost any body of water, even a small pond.

• Most waterfowl have departed, though a few Ruddy Ducks may remain. Early May is a good time to find something unexpected, however, so check lakes and ponds thoroughly for such local rarities as scoters.

• Raptors such as Osprey and Northern Harriers are still moving through, and rarities such as Mississippi Kite occasionally turn up. Early in the month, make frequent checks of the Potomac River near the mouth of Seneca Creek (Riley's Lock).

• Ring-necked Pheasant and Northern Bobwhite, both getting dif-ficult to find in the county, seem to call more this month. Scout River Road extended, past Hughes Hollow, or Triadelphia Lake Road.

• Rails, too, are difficult to find in the county, but early May is the time to search. Stop by Hughes Hollow for migrant Virginia Rail, Sora, and Common Moorhen.

- Shorebirds come through early to mid-month and include both yellowleg species, as well as Solitary, Spotted, and Least sandpipers. Spotted prefers rock outcrops near water but will settle in almost anywhere, while the others prefer muddy edges of ponds and reservoirs. Local rarities such as Long-billed Dowitcher sometimes show up this month, too, so screen carefully.

- Both cuckoo species come in this month. Black-billed is rather uncommon; only Yellow-billed will remain to breed in any numbers.

- Common Nighthawks generally pass through from mid-month onward, though mild weather may induce them to show up earlier. They sometimes call during the day from a roost tree.

- Both Chimney Swifts and Ruby-throated Hummingbirds come back in numbers by mid-month.

- Flycatchers to look for include Eastern Wood-Pewee, Acadian, Willow, Least, and Great Crested flycatchers, Eastern Kingbird, and the locally rare Olive-sided and Yellow-bellied flycatchers.

- Blue Jays, and to a lesser extent American and Fish crows, move through early in the month. Blue Jays, in loose flocks of 40 to 60 birds or more, often pass overhead from early until mid-morning.

- Vireos now on the scene include White-eyed (many of which arrived in April), Blue-headed, Yellow-throated, Warbling, Red-eyed, and an occasional Philadelphia. Good places to look for all but Warbling are Tucker Lane along the Patuxent River and Meadowside Nature Center. Warbling Vireo is fairly reliable at Layhill Park and along the canal.

- Barn and Cliff swallows return in force. The latter are reliable nesters at Brighton Dam and most years at Riley's Lock.

- Thrushes passing through from early to mid-month include Veery (which nests sporadically across the county), Swainson's, and later, Gray-cheeked and Wood thrushes. Most Hermit Thrushes have moved on; American Robins are plentiful.

- The mimic thrushes—Gray Catbird, Northern Mockingbird, and Brown Thrasher—are easily found. Meadowside Nature Center is a good place to look for all three, as is Layhill Park.

- Cedar Waxwings frequently feed on petals of early-flowering fruit trees (especially crab apple). Listen for their high-pitched calls in flight overhead.

- A host of warblers, both breeders and migrants, enliven the foliage. This is the best time to look for Blue-winged, Chestnut-sided, Magnolia, Cape May, Blackburnian, Prairie, Blackpoll, Cerulean, Prothonotary, Worm-eating, Kentucky, Mourning, Wilson's, and Canada warblers. Check any local patch of woods, especially those with good morning sun, a water feature, or both. One choice area is the canal from Pennyfield to Riley's Lock.

- Scarlet Tanagers return in early to mid-May. Summer Tanagers, rare in the county, turn up occasionally. Try Seneca Creek State Park.

- Blue Grosbeak, another locally uncommon bird, is sometimes sighted along the canal and at Hughes Hollow and Triadelphia Lake Road. Rose-breasted Grosbeak can turn up anywhere in deciduous woods and even at sunflower feeders. Indigo Buntings are back, too. Examine weedy edges of woods or shrubby fields near woodlots.

- Sparrows to look for include Chipping, Savannah, Grasshopper (increasingly hard to find), Lincoln's, and White-crowned. White-throated Sparrows have generally departed by mid-month; the south fields at Layhill Park can be especially productive.

- Bobolinks pass through in early to mid-May, peaking around the second week. A reliable place to see and hear them is at the west end of Triadelphia Lake Road.

- Triadelphia Lake Road is also a good place to look for Eastern Meadowlarks, which are becoming scarce in the county.

JUNE

- Compared with April and May, birding in June can be rather slow. Still, there are some late migrants that are usually easier to find this month, including both cuckoo species. Yellow-billed, especially, is frequently heard. Check riverside trees across the county, Hughes Hollow, and Meadowside Nature Center.

- Several flycatchers are later migrants, and they are all very vocal at this season. Look for Eastern Wood-Pewee, Great Crested Flycatcher, both Acadian and Willow flycatchers and, more rarely, Olive-sided and Yellow-bellied flycatchers. Study dead snags near water at Hughes Hollow, Ednor Road at Brown's Bridge, and along the canal.

- Warbling Vireos, which can be hard to find in Montgomery County, are more vocal now; it helps to learn their song. Check the streamside woods at Layhill Park, or anywhere along the Potomac River upstream from Pennyfield Lock.

- Blue Grosbeaks and Indigo Buntings are vocalizing, too. Listen at Hughes Hollow for both species.

- Most local breeders are singing on territory, and it pays to learn their songs, using tapes or CDs. Recognizing their songs helps you locate familiar birds; an unfamiliar song can alert you to the presence of an unusual visitor.

- Another good way to learn bird songs and still get some birding into your schedule is to volunteer to help with a breeding bird survey. M-NCPPC usually runs these informal surveys in one or two parks every summer.

JULY

- The heat and humidity of July can drain a lot of the fun out of birding, but if you get out early in the morning you can have some pleasant and rewarding days. Early-nesting species already have young fledged and out of the nest, many begging food from harried adults.

- From mid-month on, check ponds and reservoirs for egrets and herons. After nesting, many adults wander widely, and immatures disperse to feed. Make frequent visits to Hughes Hollow.

- Scan muddy edges of ponds and lakes, especially in dry summers, for early-migrating shorebirds. Both yellowlegs, as well as Semipalmated, Least, and Pectoral sandpipers, can sometimes be found, mostly in worn adult plumage. The upper reaches of Triadelphia Reservoir and the waters below Brighton Dam, such as Brown's Bridge, can be productive, as can farm fields west of Poolesville.

- For a nice change of pace, try some early evening birding. A surprising amount of feeding activity can occur after midday, and just before dusk many birds, especially the thrushes (Veery, Wood Thrush), will sing. Listen, too, for owls and Whip-poor-will at dusk; try Little Bennett Regional Park. Consult the MCC/MOS web site for summer evening field trips, usually scheduled for late-afternoon/evening on Thursdays.

- Ruby-throated Hummingbirds can be more active at feeders, especially during and after late afternoon thunderstorms. Clean feeders every day or two during hot weather.

- Most Orchard Orioles will be gone by month's end.

AUGUST

- Though some birds are on the move as early as July, autumn migration really gets under way in August, particularly late in the month.

- Watch for long-legged waders at local ponds and reservoirs. Many young birds turn up, and the chances for something uncommon such as Tricolored Heron or White or Glossy Ibis increase as the birds disperse from nesting sites. Check Hughes Hollow especially.

- Blue-winged Teal, an early migrant, can turn up by month's end on local waterways, usually in small numbers.

- Osprey migration begins this month and will continue through mid-October or even later. Northern Harriers pass through from late August into September. It pays to scan the skies for passing raptors, honing your skills in preparation for the coming season. The day or two following the passage of a cold front, with blue skies and puffy cumulus clouds, can be most productive.

- Sightings of Ring-necked Pheasant, Wild Turkey, and Northern Bobwhite—all uncommon in the county—seem to increase this month. Adults with young are sometimes encountered in their dwindling habitat. Check River Road between Hughes Hollow and White's Ferry, as well as Triadelphia Lake Road.

- August can be a good month for local rarities, such as Common Moorhen, Sandhill Crane, and Stilt Sandpiper.

- Shorebirds can show up in good numbers wherever mudflats are exposed by low water levels. Semipalmated Plovers, both yellowlegs, and Semipalmated, Western, Least, and Pectoral sandpipers can be found in dry summers. Brown's Bridge can be productive, especially in late afternoon light.

- Laughing Gulls and Caspian Terns both begin passing through in small numbers by month's end. Check larger bodies of water.

- Yellow-billed Cuckoos, mostly silent now, are more numerous this month and into early September.

- Common Nighthawks, which begin their migration south late in the month, emerge toward dusk. They frequently skim ponds for insects, allowing good, close views.

- Some of the flycatchers are more in evidence: Yellow-bellied appear in small numbers by the end of the month; Acadian still call from wet deciduous woods. Great Crested Flycatcher and Eastern Kingbird are mostly gone by month's end. Check dead snags, especially along the canal and at Hughes Hollow, for Olive-sided Flycatcher.

- Any of the eastern vireos can be seen in August, though Warbling and Yellow-throated are mostly gone by the end of the month. White-eyed and Red-eyed are still singing.

- Swallow flocks swell this month, especially near water. Check trees as well as overhead wires near Hughes Hollow for Tree, Northern Rough-winged, and Bank swallows. Study plumages carefully; many birds will be immatures.

- Look and listen for Blue-gray Gnatcatchers, wandering in small groups, early to mid-month.

- The first warblers to depart are Yellow-throated, Cerulean, Prothonotary, and Louisiana Waterthrush. In late August look for passing Blue-winged, early Magnolia, Blackburnian, American Redstart, Canada, and, more rarely, Mourning. The bulk of the migrants pass through in September.

- Blue Grosbeak, never common in the county, can be seen in small numbers. The best place to look, Hughes Hollow, has many acres of prime habitat. Indigo Buntings are fairly plentiful; check Meadowside Nature Center, Little Bennett, and Hughes Hollow.

SEPTEMBER

- Fall migration proceeds in earnest. September can rival April and May for variety and numbers of birds.

- Blue-winged Teal numbers peak in the first two weeks.

- Osprey continue coming through. Most Broad-winged Hawks push through by the third week. Other raptors to keep an eye out for are Sharp-shinned and Cooper's hawks and a few Red-shouldered and Red-tailed hawks, along with a strong push of American Kestrels until mid-October. A few Merlins may be seen late in the month, as well as an occasional Peregrine Falcon.

- Sora, though seldom sighted in the county, migrate through from now until the first hard frost. Search especially at Hughes Hollow, though any pond with extensive stands of cattails may hold one or two.

- Shorebirds to seek out include two uncommon "grasspipers": American Golden-Plover and Buff-breasted Sandpiper. Check the only likely habitat left, the extensive turf farms along old River Road toward White's Ferry. In dry summers, Pectoral Sandpipers may remain for at least the first two weeks of September.

- Laughing Gulls pass over in migration, though most have lost their trademark black hoods. They can be seen in small numbers, occasionally swooping up insects in flight, through at least mid-month. Ring-billed and Herring gulls start reappearing. Caspian Terns continue to pass through; check large bodies of water.

- Common Nighthawks continue to move through, mostly early in the month. Most Chimney Swifts will have disappeared by month's end. Ruby-throated Hummingbirds are almost all gone by early September.

- Be on the lookout for increasingly hard-to-find Red-headed Woodpeckers; both immatures and adults pass through in very small numbers. The earliest Yellow-bellied Sapsuckers appear about mid-month. Northern Flickers and Pileated Woodpeckers can also be more in evidence.

- Lingering flycatchers include Eastern Wood-Pewee, Least Flycatcher, many Eastern Phoebes, a few Great Crested Flycatchers, and Eastern Kingbird.

- September is the best month for vireos, with all six species possible, though most Warbling and Yellow-throated vireos will have left in late August. White-eyed, Red-eyed, and Philadelphia can be found, all in the same areas, through at least the first three weeks. Blue-headed comes in later, from mid-September until mid-October. Meadowside Nature Center provides excellent habitat.

- Small, loose flocks of Blue Jays congregate in every woodlot.

- Red-breasted Nuthatches migrate through. Though fond of pines, in migration they can be found in a variety of trees.

- The first Brown Creepers appear by mid-month.

- House Wrens are still common and very vocal early to mid-month, then become scarce. Winter Wrens can be seen along small creeks in wet tangles and roots of upturned trees as early as mid-month.

- The season's first Ruby-crowned Kinglets appear in a variety of habitats, including deciduous woods. Blue-gray Gnatcatcher numbers wane; most will be gone by month's end.

- Thrushes begin to migrate, starting with Wood Thrush and Veery, which breed here, followed by Swainson's, then Gray-cheeked and Bicknell's. Late in the month, the first Hermit Thrushes arrive. Look for thrushes in wet deciduous woods, such as the north trails at Layhill Park. Check also Seneca Creek State Park and Meadowside.

- Gray Catbird numbers swell, as migrants join the local breeders. Brown Thrashers appear too, though in smaller quantities; most are gone by month's end.

- Warblers pass through daily all month long, with numbers often soaring after the passage of a cold front. If mornings are cold, feeding activity can begin later in the day, and good finds are possible as late as midday. Look for Tennessee and Nashville (both easier to find in the county in fall), Northern Parula, Chestnut-sided, Magnolia, Black-throated Blue, Black-throated

Green, early Yellow-rumped, Blackburnian, Prairie, Palm, Bay-breasted, Blackpoll, Black-and-white, American Redstart, Worm-eating, Ovenbird, Northern Waterthrush, Kentucky, Connecticut and Mourning (both rare), Common Yellowthroat, Hooded (mostly gone), a few Wilson's (check willow trees), Canada, and Yellow-breasted Chat. Edges of woods with strong morning sunlight produce good results. Meadowside Nature Center and Tucker Lane in Ashton are both choice sites.

- Scarlet Tanagers, with males in basic plumage, pass through until the end of the month.

- Rose-breasted Grosbeaks and Indigo Buntings stay on until mid-month.

- Savannah Sparrows begin to appear by mid-September. Lincoln's Sparrows are possible this month and into next; check weedy tangles and hedgerows near water. Swamp Sparrows, early White-throated Sparrows, and Dark-eyed Juncos begin to show up late in the month. Layhill Park is one of the county's finest sparrow spots.

- Baltimore Orioles are present from early to mid-month, sometimes later. They occasionally sing snippets of song and are sometimes seen in the vicinity of their old nests.

- American Goldfinches are abundant, especially near fields of thistle such as those along Sycamore Landing Road.

OCTOBER

- October can be one of the most productive months for birding in Montgomery County. The weather is generally fair and sunny with low humidity, making for perfect birding days. Although most of the neotropical songbirds have departed, their place is taken by waterfowl, raptors, and sparrows.

- Pied-billed Grebes return in force.

- Double-crested Cormorants stage a comeback before leaving for warmer climes. Many will gather on or over the Potomac River.

- Most of the long-legged waders have moved on, but a few can still be found. American Bitterns trickle through until the end of November, though they are generally scarce. Great Blue Herons will stay in small numbers as long as they have open water. Most Great Egrets will be gone by mid-month.

- Wintering waterfowl begin to move in; most will stay until spring. Check ponds and reservoirs for Snow Goose, Wood Duck, Green-winged Teal, Northern Pintail, Northern Shoveler, Gadwall, American Wigeon, and Ruddy Duck. Check Black Hill Regional Park, Zion Road pond, and Lake Needwood.

- Raptors are moving through. By month's end, any remaining Osprey will have left. Northern Harriers come through, though never in large numbers. Sharp-shinned and Cooper's hawks can be seen in good numbers all month, as can Red-shouldered and Red-tailed hawks. American Kestrel migration peaks by mid-month, although a few will remain all winter in proper habitat.

- American Coots show up this month (although a few seem to hang around Black Hill Regional Park year-round).

- Be on the lookout for Common Snipe; check muddy edges of ponds and the wet fields along Sycamore Landing Road. You may also find a few Lesser Yellowlegs and Solitary Sandpipers.

- A few cuckoos may still be found.

- The last Chimney Swifts linger through mid-month.

- Yellow-bellied Sapsucker migration peaks in mid-month; some will stay the winter. Northern Flicker numbers are high, with groups foraging in most patches of deciduous woods.

- Most flycatchers are gone. A few Least Flycatchers may pass through in the first couple of weeks, while Eastern Phoebes can be seen throughout the month.

- A few White-eyed Vireos may linger; immatures occasionally sing this time of year. Small numbers of Blue-headed Vireos can be seen, especially in the first half of the month. The same is true of Yellow-throated and Philadelphia vireos.

- Blue Jays are plentiful until at least the end of the month.

- Tree Swallow numbers peak this month; most of the other swallows will have departed.

- Brown Creepers can be found in deciduous woods from October through March.

- House Wrens can still show up on warm days in the beginning of the month, but most will soon be gone. During the first week or two of October, migrating Marsh Wrens can be found wherever there are extensive cattail stands. Check wet woods with rooty tangles for Winter Wrens.

- Both Golden-crowned and Ruby-crowned kinglets flit about in good numbers this month and next. Look for Golden-crowned wherever you find pine trees, including Little Bennett Regional Park, Seneca Creek State Park, and Brookside Nature Center. Ruby-crowned can be spotted anywhere.

- Although most thrush migration is past, Veery and Gray-cheeked and Swainson's thrushes may still be around early in the month. Wintering Hermit Thrush arrive in earnest from mid-month onward. Check Layhill Park, Little Bennett, and Seneca Creek.

- Gray Catbird migration falls off dramatically, though a few cat-birds will remain if weather is mild, and one or two may over-winter. Brown Thrashers are fewer than ever.

- Small roving bands of Cedar Waxwings can be seen and heard throughout the county from now until about mid-December, when numbers taper off.

- Except for Yellow-rumped Warbler, which regularly winters here, the last remaining warblers pass through. Look for Tennessee, Nashville, Northern Parula, Orange-crowned (rare), Magnolia, Black-throated Blue, Black-throated Green, Palm, Blackpoll, Black-and-white, American Redstart, Connecticut (rare), and Common Yellowthroat. Most of these will be gone by mid-month, though a few Orange-crowned may spend the win-ter. There are also scattered records of individuals of several species that have overwintered: Black-throated Blue, Palm, Black-and-white, Ovenbird, Common Yellowthroat, and Yellow-breasted Chat.

- Scarlet Tanager can be found, but not much later than the sec-ond week. The same is true of Rose-breasted Grosbeak and Indigo Bunting.

- If you like sparrows, October is your month. Many return to our area to spend the winter, while some local breeders remain and migrants move through. Check weedy fields and low, wet areas of edge habitat for Eastern Towhee and Chipping, Field, Savannah, Song, Lincoln's (rare), Swamp, White-throated, and White-crowned sparrows, plus Dark-eyed Junco. Little Bennett, Layhill, and Lake Needwood are good spots.

- A few Baltimore Orioles remain through month's end. Rusty Blackbird numbers begin to increase from mid-month on, especially in wet woods; check Hughes Hollow and damp sections of the canal.

- Fill your bird feeders to help migrants refuel and to attract winter visitors. Remember to sprinkle millet on the ground for doves, sparrows, and other ground feeders.

NOVEMBER

- The blustery days of November, with mostly sunny skies and cooler temperatures, can be very productive for waterfowl and raptors and, to a lesser extent, sparrows.

- Common Loons migrate through; they often fly fairly low and are almost always an early-morning migrant. Have a look at Black Hill Regional Park or Triadelphia Reservoir.

- Horned Grebes join increasing numbers of Pied-billed Grebes. Check the Potomac River along the canal and Black Hill.

- A few Double-crested Cormorants may linger through at least mid-month.

- Tundra Swans migrate into our area from about mid-month onward. Other newly arriving waterfowl include American Black and Ring-necked ducks, Greater and Lesser scaup, Common Goldeneye, Bufflehead, and Hooded Merganser. All of these species can be found at Black Hill, the county's premier hotspot for waterfowl.

- A windy November day can produce good numbers of both vulture species as well as raptors. Osprey can still be found. Bald Eagles, strong flyers, are often seen this month, flying into the wind. Northern Harrier and Sharp-shinned, Cooper's, Red-shouldered, and Red-tailed hawks can all be spotted. Sightings of American Kestrel—and more rarely Merlin—are possible.

This is also the best month for wandering Northern Goshawk and Golden Eagle. Although the county has no organized hawk-watch, any open spot with a clear, unobstructed view of the sky can be productive.

- Check muddy pond edges for lingering shorebirds, though Common Snipe is the only one likely.

- Owls can be more vocal this month. Listen for Eastern Screech-Owl and Great Horned Owl at dawn and dusk. Barred Owls will often call during the day when it is overcast.

- Belted Kingfishers, found year-round throughout the county, are heard and seen in good numbers.

- An occasional White-eyed or Red-eyed vireo may hang on into the first days of November, while Blue-headed Vireo may linger through mid-month.

- Fish Crows join flocks of American Crows in winter roosts. Listen for their nasal "kah-ah" call as they stream overhead.

- Winter Wren can be found skulking around exposed roots along creek banks and shrubby areas near water, including the canal.

- Along with abundant Yellow-rumped Warblers, you may find a lingering Common Yellowthroat or, rarely, an Orange-crowned Warbler.

- Most Fox Sparrows arrive during November. Dense weedy thickets along the edges of woods are the preferred habitat. Layhill Park and the north end of Lake Needwood are good places to search.

- Rusty Blackbirds can still be found, especially in wet woods. Check at Hughes Hollow.

- Now that the weather is reliably cool, set out suet to attract woodpeckers, nuthatches, and a surprising variety of other birds. Squirrels are less likely to go after plain suet or suet mixed with insects.

DECEMBER

- Waterfowl numbers and variety are like November's. New arrivals include an occasional Redhead, usually in the company of Canvasbacks, and both Common and Red-breasted mergansers. These latter two frequent Triadelphia Reservoir.

- American Coot numbers peak between the end of November and the middle of December.

- Owl roosts can be easier to locate now that the leaves have fallen. Check under stands of evergreens for whitewash or pellets, both signs of an owl roost. Northern Saw-whet Owls prefer stands of conifers in woods or tangles of honeysuckle vines. Long-eared Owls prefer dense stands of conifers near open areas (such as at tree nurseries). Get permission to search on private property.

- A few Red-breasted Nuthatches can be found in most winters. This time of year they stick to their preferred habitat, pine trees. Try Little Bennett Regional Park.

- Winter Wren and Hermit Thrush are present in small numbers.

- The new sparrow arrival this month is the handsome American Tree Sparrow; small numbers can be seen in mixed sparrow flocks. Visit the Agricultural History Farm Park.

- Though never common, Purple Finches increase in number this month. They can be alone in the woods or mixed in with House Finches and American Goldfinches. Check the tops of tulip poplar trees (whose seeds they eat) in mixed woods.

- To enjoy early winter birding to its fullest, volunteer for one of the area's four Christmas Bird Counts, sponsored by the National Audubon Society. To find out more about the counts, check the MCC/MOS web site. Y

—Rick Sussman

Species Accounts

A total of 319 species of birds have been recorded in Montgomery County, 251 regularly occurring and 68 accidentals. The regularly occurring species, including breeders, are discussed here.

Red-throated Loon. Rare March to mid-April and late October to mid-December. Large lakes such as Triadelphia Reservoir or, more likely, the Potomac River above the rapids at Violette's Lock.

Common Loon. Uncommon late March to mid-May and late September to early December; possible through the winter. Often seen flying overland in the spring. Usually on the Potomac above Violette's Lock; also on large lakes, especially Black Hill and Triadelphia Reservoir.

Pied-billed Grebe. Common mid-August to early May. Small ponds to large lakes, Hughes Hollow and the Potomac above Violette's Lock.

Horned Grebe. Occasional from mid-October to early February; uncommon through early May. Generally on the Potomac above Violette's Lock or at Black Hill.

Red-necked Grebe. Rare. Seen after deep freezes to the north force them south in January or February. Black Hill or the Potomac or any of its open tributaries.

Double-crested Cormorant. Common early March to late November, especially Watkins Island in the Potomac upstream from Swain's Lock and also at Triadelphia Reservoir.

American Bittern. Occasional late March to early May and late September to early December. Marshes, especially Hughes Hollow or Sycamore Landing.

Least Bittern. Occasional early April to early October. Has bred at Hughes Hollow. Listen for its cu-cu-cu call in summer.

Great Blue Heron. Common year-round. Streams and pond edges. Breeds on Watkins Island in the Potomac upstream from Swain's Lock.

Great Egret. Uncommon mid-March through June; common July to mid-October at Hughes Hollow, the Pennyfield ponds or edges of large lakes.

Snowy Egret. Occasional April to mid-October. Hughes Hollow.

Little Blue Heron. Rare in spring, but occasional through mid-September. at Hughes Hollow and Ednor Road at Brown's Bridge.

Green Heron. Common April through September. Edges of small ponds, streams, and lakes. Breeds at Hughes Hollow.

Black-crowned Night-Heron. Uncommon April through September. Breeders from the National Zoo area feed on islands in the Potomac, occasionally to Hughes Hollow.

Yellow-crowned Night-Heron. Occasional April through September. Has bred at Sycamore Landing, Dickerson, and Sligo Creek. Seen annually at Hughes Hollow.

Glossy Ibis. Rare spring migrant. Has been seen at Hughes Hollow in late summer.

Turkey Vulture. Common year-round. Open country, but birds from the National Zoo area follow Wisconsin Avenue daily to feed in the upper county. A roost is located along Route 28 west of Route 124.

Black Vulture. Common resident. Open country, frequently soaring above Turkey Vultures. Seen along the Canal.

Greater White-fronted Goose. Rare October to mid-April. Seen with flocks of migrant Canada Geese grazing in open fields.

Snow Goose. Occasional October to April. Generally with flocks of migrant Canada Geese grazing in open fields.

Canada Goose. Common permanent resident. Migrants arrive in October, leave in April. Graze on golf courses and other grassy expanses, and on corn stubble.

Mute Swan. Rare fall through spring. Large lakes.

Tundra Swan. Uncommon late October through March. Black Hill, Zion Road Pond, or the Potomac.

Wood Duck. Common late February through October; occasional in mild winters. Ponds, streams and swamps such as those along the Potomac, especially Hughes Hollow, Sycamore Landing, Little Bennett, and Black Hill.

Gadwall. Uncommon mid-October to mid-April. Ponds or large lakes.

American Wigeon. Uncommon mid-August through early May. Ponds and large lakes.

American Black Duck. Common, more so in winter. Often with Mallards in the same habitat; large lakes, Hughes Hollow.

Mallard. Common resident. Almost any pond or stream.

Blue-winged Teal. Uncommon late March to early May; rare in summer; occasional August to early October. Regular in spring at the Pennyfield ponds, Hughes Hollow and Black Hill.

Northern Shoveler. Occasional September to April. Ponds, lakes and swamps along the Potomac, as well as the river itself.

Northern Pintail. Uncommon mid-September to early December; occasional through the end of April. Ponds and lakes.

Green-winged Teal. Common mid-March to early May; uncommon August to mid-November; less likely in winter. Ponds and lakes; regular at the Pennyfield ponds, Hughes Hollow, and Black Hill.

Canvasback. Uncommon November through mid-April. Regular at Black Hill and Zion Road pond.

Redhead. Ranges from rare in October to occasional in winter to uncommon in spring (April). The most consistent locations are Black Hill and the Potomac above Violette's Lock.

Ring-necked Duck. Common October through April on large lakes and ponds.

Greater Scaup. Occasional October to February; rare March and April. Large lakes and the Potomac above Violette's Lock.

Lesser Scaup. Common October and November; uncommon in winter through early May. Larger lakes and the Potomac above Violette's Lock.

Surf Scoter. Rare in late winter. Large lakes and particularly on the Potomac.

White-winged Scoter. Rare in late winter. Large lakes and particularly on the Potomac.

Black Scoter. Rare in late winter. Large lakes and particularly on the Potomac.

Long-tailed Duck. Occasional mid-October to early May, more common in spring. Large lakes and the Potomac above Violette's Lock.

Bufflehead. Common mid-October to mid-May. Ponds, lakes and the Potomac.

Common Goldeneye. Uncommon November to April, except occasional in winter. Larger lakes, especially Black Hill.

Hooded Merganser. Common November to May; occasional in summer. Ponds and lakes; best places are Black Hill, Lake Needwood, and Hughes Hollow, the latter particularly in the spring.

Common Merganser. Uncommon in November; common December to April. Large lakes and the Potomac, particularly at Violette's Lock.

Red-breasted Merganser. Uncommon mid-October to December and March to mid-May; occasional in winter. Large lakes and the Potomac.

Ruddy Duck. Common mid-September to February; uncommon to early June. Large lakes.

Osprey. Common March to May and September and October; uncommon in summer. Larger lakes and the Potomac.

Bald Eagle. Uncommon year-round. Nests at Great Falls and elsewhere down the Potomac as well as at Triadelphia Reservoir. Frequents Black Hill in winter.

Northern Harrier. Uncommon September to May, except occasional in winter. Requires extensive open fields or marshes.

Sharp-shinned Hawk. Common September to May. Woodland edges and suburban feeders.

Cooper's Hawk. Uncommon September to May; occasional in summer. Woodlands; sometimes raids feeders. May breed at Seneca Creek State Park.

Northern Goshawk. Rare November to February. Woodlands along streams such as Seneca Creek; also at Hughes Hollow and Sycamore Landing.

Red-shouldered Hawk. Common year-round in mature woodlands, especially Hughes Hollow.

Broad-winged Hawk. Common migrant early April to May and late August to early October; occasional breeder in isolated woodlots. Look at high clouds with your binoculars in September. Check edges of deciduous woods in the morning during migration, especially Little Bennett.

Red-tailed Hawk. Common year-round. Prefers fields, but now frequents suburbs with mature trees.

Rough-legged Hawk. Rare October to April; a winter visitor in open country following heavy snow cover to the north.

Golden Eagle. Rare October to February. Most sightings just inland from the Potomac.

American Kestrel. Formerly common spring through fall; now uncommon throughout the year. Perches on power lines in open farm country.

Merlin. Occasional throughout the year. Woodland edges where migrant passerines are concentrated. Recently has wintered in Silver Spring.

Peregrine Falcon. Rare migrant in April and October, but may linger through the winter on large buildings in Bethesda.

Ring-necked Pheasant. Rare resident, virtually extirpated from farmland, but may hold out near Hughes Hollow or Triadelphia Lake Road.

Wild Turkey. Uncommon resident, but increasingly regular in lowlands along the Potomac. In the spring, listen at dawn at Hughes Hollow, Sycamore Landing, Black Hill, or Triadelphia Reservoir.

Northern Bobwhite. Rare resident, virtually extirpated from farmlands, but may persist near Sycamore Landing, Triadelphia Lake Road, and up-county near the canal in Dickerson Conservation Area.

King Rail. Rare April to early October. Marshes such as Hughes Hollow.

Virginia Rail. Rare mid-March to October. Marshes such as Hughes Hollow.

Sora. Uncommon mid-April to late May and mid-August to mid-October. Marshy edges of lakes and ponds with cattails such as Hughes Hollow, stormwater management ponds, or even streamlets in corn fields.

Common Moorhen. Uncommon April to July; rare August to September. Marsh edges; Hughes Hollow.

American Coot. Common October to May on lakes and ponds and on the Potomac above Violette's Lock; numerous in winter at Black Hill.

Black-bellied Plover. Rare migrant in May and from August to November. Mud flats or turf farms.

American Golden-Plover. Rare in April; occasional late August to mid-November. Extensive short grass, turf farms.

Semipalmated Plover. Rare May; occasional June to August. Wet mud flats around lakes and ponds or even in wet farm fields. Try Ednor Road at Brown's Bridge.

Killdeer. Common year-round in short grass or gravel and muddy edges of lakes and ponds. Try farm fields and turf farms.

Greater Yellowlegs. Uncommon; primarily April and May, July to October. Edges of lakes, wet spots in farm fields or turf farms.

Lesser Yellowlegs. Uncommon; primarily April and May, July to September. Edges of lakes, wet spots in farm fields or turf farms.

Solitary Sandpiper. Uncommon April and May, July to September. Shallow streams and pond edges. Regular at the Pennyfield ponds in spring.

Spotted Sandpiper. Common mid-April to October. Streams and pond edges; numerous on rocks in the Potomac River near Carderock and Blockhouse Point in May.

Upland Sandpiper. Rare mid-April to mid-September. Extensive dry fields with short or tall grass, turf farms.

Semipalmated Sandpiper. Occasional mid-April to mid-June and mid-July to October; rare in midsummer. Mud flats on the edges of ponds and lakes or flooded fields. Try Ednor Road.

Western Sandpiper. Rare July to October. Mud flats on the edges of ponds and lakes or wet spots in turf farms.

Least Sandpiper. Uncommon April and May, July and August. Mud flats on edges of ponds and lakes; also wet spots in farm fields or turf farms. Try Ednor Road.

White-rumped Sandpiper. Rare mid-August to October. Mud flats on edges of ponds and lakes.

Baird's Sandpiper. Rare mid-August to October. Grassy mud on the edges of ponds, turf farms.

Pectoral Sandpiper. Occasional late March to mid-May, mid-July to October. Mud flats on lake edges, wet spots on turf farms. Try Ednor Road.

Dunlin. Rare September to November. Mud flats on edges of lakes.

Buff-breasted Sandpiper. Rare July to mid-October. Extensive grassy fields, turf farms.

Short-billed Dowitcher. Rare July to early October. Shallow water at pond edges.

Common Snipe. Common late February to mid-May; uncommon September to November; occasional in winter. Marshy pond edges, drainage ditches, wet meadows. Regular at Hughes Hollow and in wet fields along Sycamore Landing Road.

American Woodcock. Uncommon February to November; rare in winter. Display begins in February and continues into May in fields near wet woods, particularly along River Road at Hughes Hollow, or further up-county between Edward's Ferry and White's Ferry Roads.

Laughing Gull. Rare throughout the year. Migrants could occur along the Potomac. September migrant along the Patuxent River.

Bonaparte's Gull. Common migrant mid-March through April; occasional mid-September to mid-December along the Potomac, especially at Riley's Lock; irregular throughout the winter.

Ring-billed Gull. Common throughout the year except in summer. Frequents the Potomac as well as shopping mall parking lots; most numerous in migration.

Herring Gull. Common throughout the year, except rare in summer, particularly along the Potomac.

Great Black-backed Gull. Common mid-October to February; uncommon March to early May along the Potomac or at Brighton Dam.

Caspian Tern. Common mid-April to mid-May, occasional in summer and uncommon August to mid-October. Migrates along the Potomac and seen at Triadelphia Reservoir.

Common Tern. Rare in spring and fall when other terns are migrating along the Potomac.

Forster's Tern. Occasional late March through November. Migrates along the Potomac.

Black Tern. Occasional in May and from mid-July to mid-September on the Potomac. Rare in summer.

Rock Dove. Common all year in urban areas and around barnyards.

Mourning Dove. Common all year from suburbs to farmland.

Black-billed Cuckoo. Uncommon May, rare June and July, uncommon August to early October. Woodland edges, second-growth forests, orchards, and fruit trees with tent caterpillars. Try Little Bennett.

Yellow-billed Cuckoo. Common May through October in wooded areas, orchards, and fruit trees with tent caterpillars. Try Little Bennett.

Barn Owl. Rare throughout the year. Nearly extirpated from the county. Can be heard migrating at night in September and October.

Eastern Screech-Owl. Common. Deciduous woodlots, especially near streams; large gardens. Try Mt. Ephraim Road, Lake Needwood.

Great Horned Owl. Common year-round in mature woods, particularly pines; frequents the outer suburbs.

Barred Owl. Common year-round in mature bottomlands such as at Hughes Hollow or Riley's Lock; adapts to humans.

Long-eared Owl. Rare late October to April. Likes isolated, dense conifers or stands of conifers near open fields, such as at tree farms or nurseries.

Short-eared Owl. Rare November to mid-April in extensive grassy meadows and open farmlands.

Northern Saw-whet Owl. Rare mid-October to November and in March; occasional in winter. Small, dense conifers near clearings.

Common Nighthawk. Rare breeder; uncommon migrant in May, common August to September. Large numbers overhead on late August evenings.

Whip-poor-will. Uncommon mid-April to September. Woodlots in open farmland. Best heard in May. Try the campground area in Little Bennett or Mt. Ephraim Road.

Chimney Swift. Common early April to mid-October. Familiar summer sound overhead.

Ruby-throated Hummingbird. Common late April to early October in woods near water. Red flowers in gardens attract them to nearby feeders. Keep feeders up into the winter to attract vagrants, perhaps western species such as Rufous.

Belted Kingfisher. Common year-round. Lakes and ponds, but especially moving water. No stream or pond is too small.

Red-headed Woodpecker. Occasional year-round. Open stands of dead trees. Try Riley's Lock, Hughes Hollow, Sycamore Landing Road, or the east end of the lake at Black Hill.

Red-bellied Woodpecker. Common resident. Mature deciduous trees in woods or suburbs.

Yellow-bellied Sapsucker. Uncommon April to mid-May and mid-September to October; common in winter. Deciduous woods near water. Many winter along the C&O Canal; check apple trees or orchards as well.

Downy Woodpecker. Common resident. Any deciduous trees; common feeder bird.

Hairy Woodpecker. Common resident. Prefers mature woodland.

Northern Flicker. Common year-round, most numerous in migration. Prefers deciduous woods, but relishes ants and often feeds on the ground.

Pileated Woodpecker. Common resident. Requires extensive mature woodland, especially along streams, but frequents older suburbs.

Olive-sided Flycatcher. Rare in May; occasional in late August and September. Dead snags in open areas of mature woods near water. Try Hughes Hollow, Riley's or Violette's Locks.

Eastern Wood-Pewee. Common May to mid-October in mature deciduous woodland.

Yellow-bellied Flycatcher. Rare May to early June; occasional August to mid-October. Likes moist woods, swamps.

Acadian Flycatcher. Common late April to September in deciduous woodlands near streams. Breeds along the canal, Rock Creek, Seneca Creek, Watts Branch.

Alder Flycatcher. Rare May to late September. Shrubs in wetlands such as at Hughes Hollow; deciduous wood edges.

Willow Flycatcher. Uncommon May to September. Breeds at Hughes Hollow and possibly in streamside fields in Little Bennett.

Least Flycatcher. Occasional in May and mid-August to September. Edges of deciduous woods. Calls in spring.

Eastern Phoebe. Common early March to early November. A few may winter. Deciduous wood edges, especially near moving water.

Great Crested Flycatcher. Common late April to August; occasional to late September. Mature deciduous woods.

Eastern Kingbird. Common late April to late September. Open areas near streams.

White-eyed Vireo. Common mid-April to mid-October. Brushy edges and second growth.

Yellow-throated Vireo. Uncommon May to September. Mature deciduous bottomland such as the Potomac valley, Little Bennett, or Tucker Lane along the Patuxent River.

Blue-headed Vireo. Common April and May; uncommon September and October. Deciduous wood edges. Try Kingsley Trail at Little Bennett.

Warbling Vireo. Common late April to May; uncommon to late September. Mature deciduous trees near water, especially along the Potomac from Carderock to Sycamore Landing and in Layhill Park.

Philadelphia Vireo. Rare May; uncommon late August to mid-October. Woodlot edges near streams. Try Meadowside Nature Center or Tucker Lane.

Red-eyed Vireo. Common mid-April to late October. Deciduous woods; sings incessantly.

Blue Jay. Common year-round. Large numbers overhead in migration mid-April to early May and late September to late October. Mature oaks anywhere.

American Crow. Common resident. In winter large roost at White Flint Mall, Rockville, fans out in long, strung-out flocks each morning to feed in outer suburbs and upper county farmland, returning in the evening.

Fish Crow. Common resident. About ten percent of the White Flint crow roost; last flocks in spring and first flocks in fall consist entirely of Fish Crows. Prefers to be near water.

Common Raven. Rare resident. Nearest breeders are at Sugarloaf Mountain, Frederick County. Occasionally wanders.

Horned Lark. Occasional year-round. Upper county plowed fields, corn stubble. Try the intersection of Sugarland and Montevideo Roads in winter.

Purple Martin. Common mid-March to late September. Common migrant on the Potomac in spring.

Tree Swallow. Common mid-March to mid-November. Breeds at Hughes Hollow and the Agricultural Farm Park.

Northern Rough-winged Swallow. Common April to late October. Breeds along the Potomac at Pennyfield and Dickerson; migrant along the Potomac and at Hughes Hollow. Try River Road at Willard Road in fall migration.

Bank Swallow. Uncommon mid-April to mid-September. Often in mixed flocks in May over the Potomac, particularly at Blockhouse Point and Carderock. Try River Road at Willard Road in fall migration.

Cliff Swallow. Uncommon mid-April to mid-September. Blockhouse Point in May. Has bred at Lake Needwood and at Brighton Dam and recently under the aqueduct at Riley's Lock.

Barn Swallow. Common late March to early October. Open farm country.

Carolina Chickadee. Common resident in deciduous woods.

Tufted Titmouse. Common resident in deciduous woods.

Red-breasted Nuthatch. Irruptive migrant; generally uncommon September to March, occasional to early May. Prefers pines. Little Bennett, Black Hill, and Seneca Creek State Park near Clopper Lake.

White-breasted Nuthatch. Common resident in deciduous woods.

Brown Creeper. Rare breeder; uncommon rest of year in deciduous woods.

Carolina Wren. Common resident in deciduous woods and edges.

House Wren. Common mid-April to mid-October. A few overwinter. Tangles on edges of deciduous woods, gardens.

Winter Wren. Uncommon October to April in deciduous woods near water. Try Hughes Hollow, stream valleys such as the canal above Pennyfield and Riley's Locks, or the Ten-mile Creek area at Black Hill.

Sedge Wren. Rare spring and fall migrant in swampy, grassy field edges. Has been seen in mid-May in Layhill Park.

Marsh Wren. Rare migrant in cattails and tall grassy marshes, such as at Hughes Hollow.

Golden-crowned Kinglet. Common late September to mid-March in coniferous or deciduous woods. Try Black Hill or Little Bennett.

Ruby-crowned Kinglet. Common mid-September to late May in any coniferous or deciduous woods.

Blue-gray Gnatcatcher. Common April to mid-August, uncommon to late September. A few linger into the winter in deciduous woods, particularly near the canal.

Eastern Bluebird. Common throughout the year in open farmland and wood edges.

Veery. Common May and September; uncommon breeder in mature deciduous stream valleys such as Watts Branch or Little Bennett.

Gray-cheeked Thrush. Occasional migrant mid-to late May, uncommon mid-September to mid-October. Mature deciduous stream valleys such as Watts Branch. Best detected by flight note on an overcast night.

Bicknell's Thrush. Occasional late May and mid-September to mid-October in mature deciduous stream valleys such as Watts Branch. Best detected by flight note on an overcast night.

Swainson's Thrush. Common May to early June; uncommon late August to October in mature deciduous stream valleys. Common night migrant with distinctive note like a spring peeper.

Hermit Thrush. Uncommon late September to mid-May in mixed woodland, holly, or rhododendron thickets, particularly along the Potomac, at Seneca Creek State Park, or at Hughes Hollow along Hunting Quarter Road.

Wood Thrush. Common (but declining) late April to mid-September, uncommon to mid-October in mature deciduous woods.

American Robin. Common late February to late November in parks and on lawns; uncommon in winter in deciduous woods, often in sizable flocks.

Gray Catbird. Common mid-April to mid-November; a few may winter. Thickets, wood edges, and hedgerows.

Northern Mockingbird. Common resident from farmland to suburb.

Brown Thrasher. Common April and May; uncommon to September; rare in winter. Thickets and wood edges. Try McKee-Beshers.

European Starling. Common resident in most habitats.

American Pipit. Uncommon October to May. Pastures, corn stubble, especially when freshly manured.

Cedar Waxwing. Common throughout the year, especially mid-April to early June and early October to late December. Large tree-top flocks on wood edges and berry-laden ornamentals.

Blue-winged Warbler. Uncommon late April to late September. Deciduous woods; breeds in second growth. Try Pennyfield, the Kingsley Trail at Little Bennett, or Triadelphia Lake Road.

Golden-winged Warbler. Occasional late April to May and August to mid-September. Wood edges, second growth. Try the Ten-mile Creek area of Black Hill, the Carderock group picnic area, or Meadowside Nature Center.

Tennessee Warbler. Uncommon late April to May and mid-August to late October. Deciduous woods and edges.

Orange-crowned Warbler. Rare late September to mid-May. Tangles, edges, or hedgerows with small trees.

Nashville Warbler. Uncommon late April to May and September to early October. Wood edges and second growth.

Northern Parula. Common mid-April to late October. Breeds in deciduous woods near water. Try Little Bennett or along the Potomac or Patuxent Rivers.

Yellow Warbler. Common mid-April to late September. Breeds in willows near water. Hughes Hollow, Woottons Mill Park, Little Bennett.

Chestnut-sided Warbler. Common late April to May and late August to early October. Wood edges and second growth.

Magnolia Warbler. Common late April to May and August to late October. Deciduous edges and second growth.

Cape May Warbler. Uncommon late April to May and late August to early November. Deciduous or coniferous woods.

Black-throated Blue Warbler. Common mid-April to early June and mid-August to late October. Lower branches of deciduous woods.

Yellow-rumped Warbler. Common mid-September to May. Deciduous woods; in winter especially at Riley's Lock and McKee-Beshers.

Black-throated Green Warbler. Common late April to May and late August to late October. Deciduous or mixed woods.

Blackburnian Warbler. Uncommon late April to late May and late August to early October. Tops of mature deciduous trees in spring, lower branches in fall.

Yellow-throated Warbler. Uncommon, but possibly increasing in numbers, late March to early August; occasional to late September. Breeds in mature sycamores along the Potomac. Try the canal at Pennyfield, Riley's Lock, or Sycamore Landing or between the I-495 bridge and Old Angler's Inn near Carderock.

Pine Warbler. Uncommon early March to July; occasional August to mid-December; rare in winter. Breeds locally in Virginia pine stands. Try White Grounds Road north of Route 28, Greenbridge Road, or Little Bennett.

Prairie Warbler. Common late April to July, uncommon to early October. Weedy or scrubby scattered second growth. Try River Road near Hughes Hollow, Triadelphia Lake Road, Meadowside Nature Center, Seneca Creek State Park, or Little Bennett.

Palm Warbler. Uncommon late March to mid-May; common early September to October; rare in winter. Wooded edges, open brushy fields.

Bay-breasted Warbler. Uncommon May to early June and late August to late October. Mature deciduous or mixed woods.

Blackpoll Warbler. Common May to mid-June and September-October. Mature deciduous trees and suburban areas in spring, more varied habitat in fall.

Cerulean Warbler. Uncommon late April to July; rare in August. Declining breeder at Blockhouse Point and Sycamore Landing at the tops of mature deciduous trees. You will hear it more often than see it. Learn its song.

Black-and-white Warbler. Common April to May and August to late October; uncommon breeder in mixed woods. Rare in winter.

American Redstart. Common but declining mid-April to late October. Deciduous understory, second growth. Breeds at the end of Sycamore Landing Road.

Prothonotary Warbler. Common mid-April to mid-August; occasional to late September. Breeds along the canal. Try Hughes Hollow, Riley's Lock, and the wet woods north of Great Falls.

Worm-eating Warbler. Uncommon late April to mid-September. Steep hill-sides in oak-hickory climax. Breeds in Little Bennett, at Triadelphia Lake Road near the reservoir, at Blockhouse Point and elsewhere along the canal.

Ovenbird. Common mid-April to late October. Mature woods with a decid-uous understory. Breeds in Little Bennett, at Tucker Lane and at Triadelphia Lake Road along cemetery trail.

Northern Waterthrush. Uncommon late April to late May and August to late October. Swamps and thickets near wooded bogs. Try the canal, Meadowside, Little Bennett, or Hughes Hollow.

Louisiana Waterthrush. Uncommon late March to July, occasional to late August. Nests on steep stream banks with deciduous woods in Little Bennett, at Tucker Lane, and along the Potomac and fast-moving tributaries. Check streams running into the canal between Carderock and Old Angler's Inn and next to the turning basin at Riley's Lock.

Kentucky Warbler. Uncommon late April to mid-August; occasional to mid-September. Moist mature deciduous woods with heavy undergrowth. Try Tucker Lane, Meadowside, Little Bennett, Triadelphia Lake Road, or the towpath at Pennyfield, Seneca, or Sycamore Landing. Listen for the song across the canal.

Connecticut Warbler. Rare in May; occasional early September to late October. Dense thickets near water; stands of jewelweed or giant ragweed; weedy edges to cornfields.

Mourning Warbler. Occasional in May and early August to early October. Dense undergrowth in moist woods. Listen for its song between Pennyfield and Blockhouse Point. Often sings from a concealed perch.

Common Yellowthroat. Common mid-April to early October; often lingers into the winter. Edges, especially near water.

Hooded Warbler. Uncommon late April to September. Heavy understory in moist woods. Breeds along Tucker Lane and at Meadowside Nature Center on wooded hillsides near the creek.

Wilson's Warbler. Occasional in May, uncommon late August to late October. Thickets, especially willows, near water. Try Pennyfield.

Canada Warbler. Uncommon late April to May and early August to early October. Eye-level undergrowth in mature deciduous woods.

Yellow-breasted Chat. Common late April to early August; occasional to October; rare in winter. Dense thickets, second growth in open country. Try Triadelphia Lake Road or River Road near McKee-Beshers. Dependable in Little Bennett, Dickerson Conservation Park, and the Ten-mile Creek area of Black Hill.

Summer Tanager. Occasional late April to May; rare June to late September. Oaks along the canal from Great Falls to Blockhouse Point.

Scarlet Tanager. Common mid-April to late October. Mature oaks and other deciduous trees.

Eastern Towhee. Common mid-March to October; uncommon in winter. Prefers leaf litter in deciduous edges.

American Tree Sparrow. Uncommon early November to February; occasional to early April. Weedy fields, brush, small trees, marshes, wet swales with alders. Try the Agricultural Farm Park.

Chipping Sparrow. Common late March to August, uncommon to early November; rare in winter. Grassy fields, lawns.

Clay-colored Sparrow. Rare mid-September to late October. Check flocks of Chipping Sparrows in weedy fields.

Field Sparrow. Common throughout the year. Brushy edges of open fields. Try the Agricultural Farm Park, Meadowside, Little Bennett, or Sycamore Landing Road.

Vesper Sparrow. Occasional early April to mid-September. Farmlands, grassy fields; Agricultural Farm Park.

Savannah Sparrow. Uncommon March to early May and September to November; rare in summer; occasional in winter. Grassy, weedy, or plowed fields.

Grasshopper Sparrow. Uncommon early April to mid-October. Grassy or fallow fields in farm country. Try the corner of Hughes and River Roads.

Nelson's Sharp-tailed Sparrow. Rare May and October. Weedy streams or ponds adjacent to corn fields.

Fox Sparrow. Uncommon early October to early April. Most likely in February and March. Wooded undergrowth or multiflora rose thickets adjacent to deciduous woods; sometimes in suburban gardens. Try the end of Lake Needwood or, after snows, on rural road edges.

Song Sparrow. Common throughout the year. Brushy edges.

Lincoln's Sparrow. Occasional May and mid-September to late November. Thickets, often near water. Try Layhill Park or McKee-Beshers.

Swamp Sparrow. Common March to May and September to November; rare in summer; occasional in winter. Marshes, brushy fields; Hughes Hollow, Sycamore Landing Road, the end of Lake Needwood, or Meadowside Nature Center.

White-throated Sparrow. Common late September to early June. Brushy undergrowth and edges.

White-crowned Sparrow. Uncommon October to mid-May. Brushy roadside edges in up-county farmland. Try Sugarland Road where it crosses Dry Seneca Creek.

Dark-eyed Junco. Common late September to early May. Edges, shrubs.

Lapland Longspur. Rare mid-October to late March in plowed fields or corn stubble, usually with large flocks of Horned Larks.

Snow Bunting. Rare mid-October to mid-March in plowed fields or corn stubble, usually with large flocks of Horned Larks.

Northern Cardinal. Common resident. Wood edges, suburban gardens.

Rose-breasted Grosbeak. Uncommon late April to May and September to late October. Tops of deciduous trees.

Blue Grosbeak. Uncommon late April to late October. Treelines and telephone lines in farm country. Try Hughes Road at River Road, Triadelphia Lake Road, or Ednor Road at Brown's Bridge.

Indigo Bunting. Common late April to late October. Telephone lines in open farmland, weedy fields, and brushy areas with small trees. Breeds along River Road and at Little Bennett.

Dickcissel. Occasional May to July, rare in fall. Has bred on West Offutt Road near Poolesville. Try Triadelphia Lake Road. Breeds regularly in nearby Frederick County.

Bobolink. Common late April to May and August to October. Flocks in alfalfa or mustard fields. Try Triadelphia Lake Road.

Red-winged Blackbird. Common throughout the year. Marshes, farm fields. Breeds at Hughes Hollow.

Eastern Meadowlark. Uncommon and rapidly declining; occasional in winter. Open fields, power lines, fence posts. Try Triadelphia Lake Road or the polo fields on Hughes Road near River Road.

Rusty Blackbird. Uncommon early October to mid-May. Swamps, wooded wetlands; Hughes Hollow and Hunting Quarter Road, or the canal bed between Violette's Lock and Pennyfield.

Common Grackle. Common throughout most of the year, but uncommon in winter. Marshes, open fields, wooded suburbs.

Brown-headed Cowbird. Common March to October; uncommon in winter. Woods, farms, suburbs.

Orchard Oriole. Common mid-April to early August; uncommon to early September. Treelines, farmyards, suburban street trees. Pennyfield, Hughes Hollow, Woottons Mill Park, Meadowside Nature Center.

Baltimore Oriole. Common late April to late September. Deciduous woods; look for hanging nests in sycamore trees over the canal at Pennyfield, also Woottons Mill Park.

Purple Finch. Occasional September to early May. Most reliable in spring or fall, but is irruptive and can be plentiful some winters at feeders and in deciduous woods.

House Finch. Common resident. Farmlands to suburbs.

Common Redpoll. Irruptive; rare November to mid-April. Brushy, weedy edges; alder and birch catkins; thistle feeders.

Pine Siskin. Occasional October to May, most often in spring or fall migration. Weedy edges, thistle, sweet gum; often with goldfinches at feeders.

American Goldfinch. Common throughout the year. Weedy fields, thistle, second growth; feeders.

Evening Grosbeak. Irruptive; rare October to early May. A few pass through each year in October-November and April-May. Deciduous woods, feeders.

House Sparrow. Common resident from farmyards to suburbs to cities.

—*Paul O'Brien*

CHECKLIST

A Birder's Guide to
Montgomery County, MD

This list, compiled by the Montgomery County Chapter of the Maryland Ornithological Society (MOS), contains seasonal abundance information for 251 species of birds that regularly occur in the county, either as winter inhabitants, summer breeders, migrants, or year-round residents. An additional 68 "accidental" species include those that have been seen only a few times in the past 20 years. The total number of bird species for the county is thus 319. Species are listed in accordance with the seventh edition of the American Ornithologists' Union (AOU) checklist.

An asterisk (*) flags each of the 121 known breeders in Montgomery County. A double asterisk (**) marks 12 species that historically bred in the county but for which there are no breeding records since 1977.

The seasons noted in the checklist are:

Spring (March, April, and May)

Summer (June and July)

Fall (August, September, October, and November)

Winter (December, January, and February)

Abundance codes for each season/species combination:

c   The bird is **common to abundant,** i.e., it should be readily seen or heard if searched for in suitable habitat.

u   The bird is **uncommon.** The bird is generally present in the county at the right time of year and in the correct habitat, but it may not be readily seen or heard due to its secretive behavior or relative scarcity.

o   The bird is **occasionally present** during the period, i.e., generally seen only a few times during any given season.

r   The bird is **rare.** Generally speaking, it is not seen every year, but often enough to be no longer considered accidental.

Blank   The bird is not thought to be present in the county during that period.

Species	SEASONAL ABUNDANCE			
	Spring	Summer	Fall	Winter
Red-throated Loon	r		r	r
Common Loon	u		u	o
Pied-billed Grebe**	c		c	c
Horned Grebe	u		o	o
Red-necked Grebe	r		r	r
Double-crested Cormorant*	c	c	c	r
American Bittern	o		o	
Least Bittern*	o	o		
Great Blue Heron*	c	c	c	c
Great Egret	u	u	c	
Snowy Egret	o	o	o	
Little Blue Heron	r	o	o	
Green Heron*	c	c	c	
Black-crowned Night-Heron	u	u	u	
Yellow-crowned Night-Heron*	o	o	o	
Glossy Ibis	r			
Black Vulture*	c	c	c	c
Turkey Vulture*	c	c	c	c
Greater White-fronted Goose	r		r	r
Snow Goose	o		o	o
Canada Goose*	c	c	c	c
Mute Swan	r		r	r
Tundra Swan	u		u	u
Wood Duck*	c	c	c	o
Gadwall	u		u	u
American Wigeon	u		u	u
American Black Duck*	c	c	c	c
Mallard*	c	c	c	c
Blue-winged Teal**	u	r	o	
Northern Shoveler	o		o	o
Northern Pintail	o		u	o
Green-winged Teal	c		u	u
Canvasback	u		u	u
Redhead	u		r	o
Ring-necked Duck	c		c	c
Greater Scaup	r		o	o
Lesser Scaup	u		c	u

Species	SEASONAL ABUNDANCE			
	Spring	Summer	Fall	Winter
Surf Scoter				r
White-winged Scoter				r
Black Scoter				r
Long-tailed Duck	o		o	o
Bufflehead	c		c	c
Common Goldeneye	u		u	o
Hooded Merganser**	c	o	c	c
Common Merganser	c		u	c
Red-breasted Merganser	u		u	o
Ruddy Duck	u		c	u
Osprey*	c	u	c	
Bald Eagle*	u	u	u	u
Northern Harrier*	u		u	o
Sharp-shinned Hawk**	c		c	c
Cooper's Hawk*	u	o	u	u
Northern Goshawk	r		r	r
Red-shouldered Hawk*	c	c	c	c
Broad-winged Hawk*	c	o	c	
Red-tailed Hawk*	c	c	c	c
Rough-legged Hawk	r		r	r
Golden Eagle			r	r
American Kestrel*	u	u	u	u
Merlin	o	o	o	o
Peregrine Falcon**	r		o	o
Ring-necked Pheasant*	r	r	r	r
Wild Turkey*	u	u	u	u
Northern Bobwhite*	r	r	r	r
King Rail*	r	r	r	
Virginia Rail**	r	r	r	
Sora	u		u	
Common Moorhen*	u	u	r	
American Coot**	c		c	c
Black-bellied Plover	r	r	r	
American Golden-Plover	r		o	
Semipalmated Plover	r	o	o	
Killdeer*	c	c	c	c
Greater Yellowlegs	u	u	u	
Lesser Yellowlegs	u	u	u	

	SEASONAL ABUNDANCE			
Species	**Spring**	**Summer**	**Fall**	**Winter**
Solitary Sandpiper	c	u	u	
Spotted Sandpiper	c	c	c	
Upland Sandpiper**	r	r	r	
Semipalmated Sandpiper	o	r	o	
Western Sandpiper		r	r	
Least Sandpiper	u	u	u	
White-rumped Sandpiper			r	
Baird's Sandpiper		r	r	
Pectoral Sandpiper	o	o	o	
Dunlin			r	
Buff-breasted Sandpiper			r	
Short-billed Dowitcher		r	r	
Common Snipe	c		u	o
American Woodcock*	u	u	u	r
Laughing Gull	r	r	r	o
Bonaparte's Gull	c		o	o
Ring-billed Gull	c	r	c	c
Herring Gull	c	r	c	c
Great Black-backed Gull	u	r	c	c
Caspian Tern	c	o	u	
Common Tern	r		r	
Forster's Tern	o	o	o	
Black Tern	o	r	o	
Rock Dove*	c	c	c	c
Mourning Dove*	c	c	c	c
Black-billed Cuckoo*	u	r	u	
Yellow-billed Cuckoo*	c	c	c	
Barn Owl *	r	r	r	r
Eastern Screech-Owl*	c	c	c	c
Great Horned Owl*	c	c	c	c
Barred Owl*	c	c	c	c
Long-eared Owl**	r		r	r
Short-eared Owl**	r		r	r
Northern Saw-whet Owl	r		r	o
Common Nighthawk*	u	r	c	
Whip-poor-will*	u	u	r	
Chimney Swift*	c	c	c	
Ruby-throated Hummingbird*	c	c	c	

Species	SEASONAL ABUNDANCE			
	Spring	Summer	Fall	Winter
Belted Kingfisher*	c	c	c	c
Red-headed Woodpecker*	o	o	o	o
Red-bellied Woodpecker*	c	c	c	c
Yellow-bellied Sapsucker	u		u	c
Downy Woodpecker *	c	c	c	c
Hairy Woodpecker*	c	c	c	c
Northern Flicker*	c	c	c	c
Pileated Woodpecker*	c	c	c	c
Olive-sided Flycatcher	r		o	
Eastern Wood-Pewee*	c	c	c	
Yellow-bellied Flycatcher	r		o	
Acadian Flycatcher *	c	c	c	
Alder Flycatcher	r	r	r	
Willow Flycatcher*	u	u	o	
Least Flycatcher	o		o	
Eastern Phoebe*	c	c	c	r
Great Crested Flycatcher*	c	c	o	
Eastern Kingbird *	c	c	c	
White-eyed Vireo*	c	c	c	
Yellow-throated Vireo*	u	u	u	
Blue-headed Vireo	c		u	
Warbling Vireo*	c	u	u	
Philadelphia Vireo	r		o	
Red-eyed Vireo*	c	c	c	
Blue Jay*	c	c	c	c
American Crow*	c	c	c	c
Fish Crow *	c	c	c	c
Common Raven	r	r	r	r
Horned Lark*	o	o	o	o
Purple Martin*	c	c	c	
Tree Swallow*	c	c	c	
Northern Rough-winged Swallow*	c	c	c	
Bank Swallow	u	u	u	
Cliff Swallow*	u	u	u	
Barn Swallow*	c	c	c	
Carolina Chickadee*	c	c	c	c
Tufted Titmouse*	c	c	c	c
Red-breasted Nuthatch	o		u	u

Species	SEASONAL ABUNDANCE			
	Spring	Summer	Fall	Winter
White-breasted Nuthatch*	c	c	c	c
Brown Creeper*	u	r	u	u
Carolina Wren*	c	c	c	c
House Wren*	c	c	c	r
Winter Wren	u		u	u
Sedge Wren	r		r	
Marsh Wren*	r	r	r	
Golden-crowned Kinglet	c		c	c
Ruby-crowned Kinglet	c		c	c
Blue-gray Gnatcatcher*	c	c	u	
Eastern Bluebird*	c	c	c	c
Veery*	u	u	u	
Gray-cheeked Thrush	o		u	
Bicknell's Thrush	o		o	
Swainson's Thrush	c		u	
Hermit Thrush	u		u	u
Wood Thrush*	c	c	u	
American Robin*	c	c	c	u
Gray Catbird*	c	c	c	r
Northern Mockingbird*	c	c	c	c
Brown Thrasher*	c	u	u	r
European Starling*	c	c	c	c
American Pipit	u		u	u
Cedar Waxwing*	c	c	c	c
Blue-winged Warbler*	u	u	u	
Golden-winged Warbler	o		o	
Tennessee Warbler	u		u	
Orange-crowned Warbler	r		r	r
Nashville Warbler	u		u	
Northern Parula*	c	c	c	
Yellow Warbler*	c	c	c	
Chestnut-sided Warbler	c		c	
Magnolia Warbler	c		c	
Cape May Warbler	u		u	
Black-throated Blue Warbler	c		c	
Yellow-rumped Warbler	c		c	c
Black-throated Green Warbler	c		c	
Blackburnian Warbler	u		u	

Species	SEASONAL ABUNDANCE			
	Spring	Summer	Fall	Winter
Yellow-throated Warbler	u	u	o	
Pine Warbler*	u	u	o	r
Prairie Warbler*	c	c	u	
Palm Warbler	u		c	r
Bay-breasted Warbler	u		u	
Blackpoll Warbler	c		c	
Cerulean Warbler*	u	u	r	
Black-and-white Warbler*	c	u	c	r
American Redstart*	c	c	c	
Prothonotary Warbler*	c	c	o	
Worm-eating Warbler *	u	u	u	
Ovenbird*	c	c	c	
Northern Waterthrush	u		u	
Louisiana Waterthrush*	u	u	o	
Kentucky Warbler*	u	u	o	
Connecticut Warbler	r		o	
Mourning Warbler	o		o	
Common Yellowthroat*	c	c	c	
Hooded Warbler*	u	u	u	
Wilson's Warbler	o		u	
Canada Warbler	u		u	
Yellow-breasted Chat*	c	c	u	r
Summer Tanager*	o	r	r	
Scarlet Tanager*	c	c	c	
Eastern Towhee*	c	c	c	u
American Tree Sparrow	o			u
Chipping Sparrow*	c	c	u	r
Clay-colored Sparrow			r	
Field Sparrow*	c	c	c	c
Vesper Sparrow*	o	o	o	
Savannah Sparrow*	u	r	u	o
Grasshopper Sparrow*	u	u	u	
Nelson's Sharp-tailed Sparrow	r		r	
Fox Sparrow	u		u	u
Song Sparrow*	c	c	c	c
Lincoln's Sparrow	o		o	
Swamp Sparrow*	c	r	c	u
White-throated Sparrow	c		c	c

Species	SEASONAL ABUNDANCE			
	Spring	Summer	Fall	Winter
White-crowned Sparrow	u		u	u
Dark-eyed Junco	c		c	c
Lapland Longspur			r	r
Snow Bunting			r	r
Northern Cardinal*	c	c	c	c
Rose-breasted Grosbeak	u		u	
Blue Grosbeak*	u	u	u	
Indigo Bunting*	c	c	c	
Dickcissel*	o	o	r	
Bobolink	c		c	
Red-winged Blackbird*	c	c	c	c
Eastern Meadowlark*	u	u	u	o
Rusty Blackbird	u		u	u
Common Grackle*	c	c	c	u
Brown-headed Cowbird*	c	c	c	u
Orchard Oriole*	c	c	u	
Baltimore Oriole*	c	c	c	
Purple Finch	o		o	o
House Finch*	c	c	c	c
Common Redpoll	r			r
Pine Siskin	o		o	o
American Goldfinch*	c	c	c	c
Evening Grosbeak	r		r	r
House Sparrow*	c	c	c	c

—John Bjerke

ACCIDENTAL SPECIES

Eared Grebe
American White Pelican
Great Cormorant
Anhinga
Cattle Egret
Tricolored Heron
White Ibis
Black-bellied Whistling-Duck
Brant
Eurasian Wigeon
King Eider
Harlequin Duck
Swallow-tailed Kite
Mississippi Kite
Ruffed Grouse
Yellow Rail
Purple Gallinule
Sandhill Crane
American Avocet
Willet
Whimbrel
Hudsonian Godwit
Marbled Godwit
Ruddy Turnstone
Sanderling
Stilt Sandpiper
Long-billed Dowitcher
Wilson's Phalarope
Red-necked Phalarope
Red Phalarope
Pomarine Jaeger
Little Gull
California Gull
Thayer's Gull

Yellow-legged Gull
Iceland (Kumlien's) Gull
Lesser Black-backed Gull
Glaucous Gull
Black-legged Kittiwake
Arctic Tern
Sooty Tern
Thick-billed Murre
Snowy Owl
Chuck-will's-widow
Rufous Hummingbird
Western Kingbird
Scissor-tailed Flycatcher
Loggerhead Shrike
Northern Shrike
Black-capped Chickadee
Boreal Chickadee
Bewick's Wren
Varied Thrush
Swainson's Warbler
Western Tanager
Spotted Towhee
Bachman's Sparrow **
Lark Sparrow
Henslow's Sparrow **
Harris's Sparrow
Black-headed Grosbeak
Painted Bunting
Yellow-headed Blackbird
Brewer's Blackbird
Pine Grosbeak
Red Crossbill
White-winged Crossbill
Hoary Redpoll

Reporting rarities:

If you believe you have found a rarity, it is important to document your sighting carefully. Write up a full description of the bird, noting in detail its appearance and behavior, and include specifics about the setting—locale, time, lighting, optics, etc. Sketches, photos, or videos are quite helpful. This material should be submitted to the Secretary of the Maryland/DC Records Committee of the MOS, Phil Davis, 2549 Vale Court, Davidsonville, MD 21035 (301–261–1084).

Selected Resources

Books:

Iliff, Marshall J., Robert F. Ringler, and James L. Stasz. *Field List of the Birds of Maryland.* ("The Yellow Book"), Maryland Avifauna, Number 2, Maryland Ornithological Society, Third Edition, May 1996.

Kirschbaum, Elliot A., ed. *A Birder's Guide to Baltimore and Baltimore County, Maryland.* The Baltimore Bird Club, a chapter of the Maryland Ornithological Society, 1998.

Miller, Stauffer. *A Guide to Bird Finding in Frederick County, Maryland.* Frederick County Chapter of the Maryland Ornithological Society, May 1993. Out of print.

Robbins, Chandler S., and Eirik A. Blom, eds. *Atlas of the Breeding Birds of Maryland and the District of Columbia.* University of Pittsburgh Press, February 1997.

Solem, Joanne K. *Birding Howard County, Maryland.* Howard County Chapter of the Maryland Ornithological Society, 1995.

Wilds, Claudia. *Finding Birds in the National Capital Area.* Smithsonian Press. Revised Edition, 1992.

Local associations:

Audubon Naturalist Society of the Central Atlantic States. ANS, a nonprofit society dedicated to the dissemination of information on natural history and the preservation of our natural resources, publishes *Audubon Naturalist News* 10 times a year. Other activities include a diverse schedule of educational programs and field trips for children and adults. ANS sponsors The Voice of the Naturalist, a weekly report of local bird sightings and upcoming field trips; call 301–652–1088 or check web site.

Address: 8940 Jones Mill Road, Chevy Chase, MD 20815. Telephone: 301–652–9188.

Web site: **http://www.Audubonnaturalist.org**

Maryland Ornithological Society. MOS is a nonprofit, statewide organization devoted to the study and enjoyment of birds. Its purpose is to promote knowledge, appreciation, and conservation of birds and bird habitat. The society publishes the quarterly journal *Maryland Birdlife* and the bimonthly newsletter *Maryland Yellowthroat*. It also maintains a system of wildlife sanctuaries and sponsors an annual conference.

Address: Cylburn Mansion, 4915 Greenspring Avenue,
             Baltimore, MD 21209.
Telephone: 800–823–0050.

Web site: **http: //www.mdbirds.org.**

Montgomery County Chapter of MOS. MCC is one of 16 local chapters of MOS. Its 300-plus members—ranging from noted birders to enthusiastic novices—come from Montgomery and neighboring Maryland counties as well as the District of Columbia and Northern Virginia. The chapter holds lively and informative monthly meetings from September through May featuring presentations on field birding, conservation, and natural history. In addition, the chapter draws on its experienced birders to present workshops on gulls, shorebirds, and sparrows. The bimonthly newsletter, *The Chat*, includes a list of the local and more far-flung field trips available throughout the year.

Address: MCC/MOS, P.O. Box 59639, Potomac, MD 20859-9639.

Web site: **http://www.mdkinc.com/mccbird**

Northern Virginia Bird Club. This chapter of the Virginia Society of Ornithology focuses primarily on field birding, sponsoring as many as three trips per week from mid-August to mid-June. A quarterly newsletter, *The Siskin*, lists the schedule of trips as well as other bird-related activities.

Address: NVBC, P.O. Box 9241, McLean, VA 22102.

Web site: **http://sitesbysteve.com/nvbc/**

Raptor Society of Metropolitan Washington. Drawing its membership from raptor enthusiasts in the greater Washington area, the society features noted speakers at its meetings, held the last Monday of every month except May and December. The society also publishes a quarterly newsletter.

Address: P.O. Box 482, Annandale, VA 22003.

Internet:

MDOsprey is an Internet-based discussion list aimed at birders and birding in Maryland.

Web site: **http://mdosprey.home.att.net**

Assistance:

To report vandalism, habitat destruction, or disturbance of birds, call U.S. Park Police at 301–949–3010.

To report illegal shooting or dog training out of season, call Maryland Department of Natural Resources (DNR) Police at 410–356–7060.

To report injured birds or dangerous animals, call the regional office of DNR, Wildlife and Heritage Division, 301–258–7308.

Rehabilitation of injured birds:

Gary Neubaum, Montgomery County raptor rehabilitator
Telephone: 301–977–8929.

Second Chance Wildlife Center, Gaithersburg
Telephone: 301–926–9453.

The following chapter members have expressed willingness to answer questions from reporters and other media professionals regarding birds and birding-related activities:

Mike Bowen	301-530-5764	dhmbowen@yahoo.com
Linda Friedland	301-983-2136	linnet@erols.com
Dick Homan	301-229-1141	HomanRL@aol.com
Lola Oberman	301-365-1058	LTobie@aol.com
Paul O'Brien	301-424-6491	PObrien776@aol.com
Andy Rabin	703-716-2923	andyrabin@mindspring.com
Rick Sussman	301-774-1185	Warblerick@aol.com

ABA Code of Birding Ethics

A Birder's Guide to
Montgomery County, MD

PRINCIPLES OF BIRDING ETHICS

Everyone who enjoys birds and birding must always respect wildlife, its environment, and the rights of others. In any conflict of interest between birds and birders, the welfare of the birds and their environment comes first.

CODE OF BIRDING ETHICS

1. Promote the welfare of birds and their environment.

1(a) Support the protection of important bird habitat.

1(b) To avoid stressing birds or exposing them to danger, exercise restraint and caution during observation, photography, sound recording, or filming.

Limit the use of recordings and other methods of attracting birds, and never use such methods in heavily birded areas, or for attracting any species that is Threatened, Endangered, or of Special Concern, or is rare in your local area.

Keep well back from nests and nesting colonies, roosts, display areas, and important feeding sites. In such sensitive areas, if there is a need for extended observation, photography, filming, or recording, try to use a blind or hide, and take advantage of natural cover.

Use artificial light sparingly for filming or photography, especially for close-ups.

1(c) Before advertising the presence of a rare bird, evaluate the potential for disturbance to the bird, its surroundings, and other people in the area, and proceed only if access can be controlled, disturbance minimized, and permission has been obtained from private landowners. The sites of rare nesting birds should be divulged only to the proper conservation authorities.

1(d) Stay on roads, trails, and paths where they exist; otherwise keep habitat disturbance to a minimum.

2. Respect the law, and the rights of others.

2(a) Do not enter private property without the owner's explicit permission.

2(b) Follow all laws, rules, and regulations governing use of roads and public areas, both at home and abroad.

2(c) Practice common courtesy in contacts with other people. Your exemplary behavior will generate goodwill with birders and non-birders alike.

3. Ensure that feeders, nest structures, and other artificial bird environments are safe.

3(a) Keep dispensers, water, and food clean and free of decay or disease. It is important to feed birds continually during harsh weather.

3(b) Maintain and clean nest structures regularly.

3(c) If you are attracting birds to an area, ensure that the birds are not exposed to predation from cats and other domestic animals, or dangers posed by artificial hazards.

4. Group birding, whether organized or impromptu, requires special care. Each individual in the group, in addition to the obligations spelled out in Items #1 and #2, has responsibilities as a group member.

4(a) Respect the interests, rights, and skills of fellow birders, as well as people participating in other legitimate outdoor activities. Freely share your knowledge and experience, except where code 1(c) applies. Be especially helpful to beginning birders.

4(b) If you witness unethical birding behavior, assess the situation, and intervene if you think it prudent. When interceding, inform the person(s) of the inappropriate action, and attempt, within reason, to have it stopped. If the behavior continues, document it, and notify appropriate individuals or organizations.

Group leader responsibilities (amateur and professional trips and tours).

4(c) Be an exemplary ethical role model for the group. Teach through word and example.

4(d) Keep groups to a size that limits impact on the environment and does not interfere with others using the same area.

4(e) Ensure that everyone in the group knows of, and practices, this code.

4(f) Learn and inform the group of any special circumstances applicable to the areas being visited (e.g., no tape recorders allowed).

4(g) Acknowledge that professional tour companies bear a special responsibility to place the welfare of birds and the benefits of public knowledge ahead of the company's commercial interests. Ideally, leaders should keep track of trip sightings, document unusual occurrences, and submit records to appropriate organizations.

PLEASE FOLLOW THIS CODE AND DISTRIBUTE AND TEACH IT TO OTHERS

The American Birding Association's Code of Birding Ethics may be freely reproduced for distribution/dissemination.

Major Sites

1. C&O: Chain Bridge
2. C&O: Carderock
3. C&O: Great Falls
4. C&O: Pennyfield Lock
5. C&O: Seneca
6. C&O: Sycamore Landing
7. C&O: Edward's Ferry
8. McKee-Beshers WMA
9. Little Bennett Regional Park
10. Black Hill Regional Park
11. Seneca Creek State Park
12. Lake Needwood/Rock Creek
13. Meadowside Nature Center
14. Layhill Park
15. Triadelphia Lake Road
16. Rachel Carson Conservation Park

Little Treasures

A. Little Falls Branch Park
B. Locust Grove Nature Center
C. Bald Eagle Watch, Great Falls
D. Upper Watts Branch Park
E. Blockhouse Point Conservation Park
F. Meditation Park
G. Back Roads
H. Gunners Lake
I. Woottons Mill Park
J. Croydon Creek Nature Center
K. Sligo Creek Park
L. Brookside Nature Center
M. Maydale Park
N. Four Gems along the Patuxent
O. Agricultural History Farm Park
P. Duck Ponds